On being a woman

*A review of research on how
women see themselves*

FAY FRANSELLA
and KAY FROST

TAVISTOCK PUBLICATIONS

First published in 1977 by
Tavistock Publications Limited
11 New Fetter Lane,
London EC4P 4EE
Printed in Great Britain by
Richard Clay (The Chaucer
Press) Ltd Bungay, Suffolk

© Fay Fransella and
Kay Frost 1977

ISBN 0 422 76070 6 (hardbound)
ISBN 0 422 76080 3 (paperback)

Contents

Acknowledgements

It is difficult to know where to start. Perhaps there is no 'right' place. The people to whom we want to extend our thanks are in no order of priority.

Heavy burdens rested on the shoulders of Kathleen McCauley and Sonia Corbett as they did most of the typing. We thank them. The library staff at the Royal Free Hospital were relentless in their pursuit of sometimes very obscure journals. We thank them. The photo-copying staff must have wondered what had hit the system as chapter after chapter came to them in the space of a very short time. We thank them.

We also feel indebted to all those in our personal lives who paid the price of knowing a working woman who, in addition to work and home, takes on the additional task of writing a book. We thank them.

The authors and publishers are grateful to the various individuals and publishers who have given permission for material to be reproduced.

Table 1 on page 27 is reprinted from 'The Sociological Structure', by F. Nye in *Working Mothers* (1974) edited by L. Hoffman and F. Nye with the permission of the publishers Jossey Bass Inc. Publishers. *Table 2* on page 32 is reprinted from *Sex Roles and Social Structure* (1970) by H. Holter with the permission of the publishers Universitetsforlaget. *Table 3* on page 36 is reprinted from 'Sex-Role Attitudes in Finland, 1966–1970', by E. Haavio-Mannila, *Journal of Social Issues* 28 (1972): 93–110, with the permission of the author. *Table 4* on page 38 is reprinted from *Occupation: Housewife* (1971) by H. Lopata with the permission of the publishers Oxford University Press. *Table 5* on page 67 is reprinted from *Classrooms Observed* (1973) by R. Nash with the permission of the publishers Routledge & Kegan Paul Ltd. *Figures 1 and 2* on pages 73 and 74 are reprinted from 'The Onset of Academic Under-achievement in Bright Children', by M. Shaw and J. McCuen, *Journal of Educational Psychology* 51 (1960): 103–8, © 1960 American Psychological Association. Reprinted by permission. *Table 6* on page 140 is reprinted from 'Women's Fantasies during Sexual Intercourse: normative and theoretical implications', by E. B. Hariton and J. Singer, *Journal of Consulting and Clinical Psychology* 42 (1972): 313–22, © 1974 American Psychological Association. Reprinted by permission. *Table 7* on page 168 is reprinted from *Health and Personal Social Services Statistics for England and Wales* (1972) with the permission of the Controller of Her Majesty's Stationery Office.

Introduction

There are many books now available about woman. She has been studied as a child, as a teenager, as a parent, as a wife, as a widow, as mentally sick, and much else besides. She has been studied as the writer of novels, as a character in novels, as a leader of men, as a general statistic, in fact, as an object.

Our main purpose is to study woman as a subject. To see what she has to say for herself rather than what others say about her. We are concerned with what it means to a woman to be a woman. But we have not gone out and conducted our own survey in which we asked a number of standard questions. Instead, we have limited ourselves to looking at what other professionals have reported in the academic literature (mainly the sociological, and psychological).

Our second purpose is to make people aware of how uncommon it is to actually ask women what they think about themselves. For if we had limited this book to reporting such studies, it would be a very short book. So we hope that anyone interested enough to read this will be encouraged to go out and make their own enquiries and so fill this gaping hole in our knowledge.

Our third purpose is a negative one. It is *not* our intention to provide an exhaustive account of all the work that has been carried out. This is not at odds with the statement that there is very little evidence about what women think of themselves. It simply means that in some areas there is a seemingly interminable amount of information and in others virtually nothing. But there has been no bias in terms of selection of items to make a feminist point. If an article or research finding furthers our knowledge about how women perceive themselves, then we have included it even if it goes against some pet theory.

There may be too many references upsetting the natural reading flow for some. But we decided on this format because, since one of our aims is to encourage people to go out and do some more investigations, they may want to look at the original articles referred to. We also deliberately decided to keep speculation to a minimum and data to a maximum. But we have commented where we felt it useful. In some chapters we have felt the need to comment in fairly general terms at the end of the chapter, while in others, it seemed to come more naturally in the text. We have not tried to write the definitive book on women's perception of themselves. So the results of studies are often mentioned without too close a look for methodological flaws.

The reason why this is not a very short book is the result of a bias. The bias is feminist. The views of the women studied are influenced by their living in a given culture. So the picture portrayed is framed by a description of the stereotypes or beliefs existing in Western culture both now and in the past. Sometimes the picture is of a very small segment of society, since that may be all the evidence that is available. A great deal of work has been conducted on the captive mass of US college students. This is interesting in its own right, but care must be taken not to generalize from this to all other sections of female society.

Another basic bias is the psychological theory that has been used to sift the evidence in a number of places. This is George Kelly's personal construct theory. As a result, there will be no interpretation of the evidence in either learning theory terms or from a psychoanalytic point of view. From the philosophical standpoint of construct theory there are no facts in life. There are only individuals' interpretations of those facts. And the interpretations will depend on the set of construct dimensions that each individual possesses. Behaviour construed as aggressive may be seen by one woman as coming from a liberated human being, but by another as a fundamental negation of womanhood. So the construct theorist tries to understand others by looking at life through their eyes.

Once again, we do not suppose that the 'facts' discussed will 'fit' every woman. They are just some pieces of evidence that have come to light about how some women view their lives.

We hope that no woman will read this book with the expectation that it will tell her what she is. Too often theorists have done just this. And too often women have believed them. The result has been to stop individual women from constructing their own theories about their own lives and their own place in society. If some women jump up in reading this book saying 'I AM NOT LIKE THAT', we shall be delighted. But we should like to think that some people will recognize themselves, and see things which reflect their own experiences, and find this helpful. And we think that hearing about other people's ideas and experiences can serve as a jumping off point in one's own explorations.

ONE

Social definitions of a woman's place

To understand why people act as they do, we need to know how they see themselves. For by their actions people set out to make sense of their lives and of their experiences. And what makes sense to one person in one way may have a very different sort of meaning for another. What is it then that makes a particular woman choose to see herself in a particular way – and act accordingly?

Our ideas about ourselves do not simply reflect self-observation. We organize, interpret, and reinterpret what we find ourselves doing, on the basis of notions we already have of what we are about. For one woman a paid job is proof of her independence; for another it is evidence that she is a good wife and mother, who can support her family; yet another might see it simply as her husband's failure to provide as he should.

These basic notions are not constructed from thin air. In every social group there are systems of beliefs, more or less shared, about the nature and appropriate behaviour of women and men.

People organize their actions in the light of their knowledge of 'how things are done'; of what they can expect of others; and of what others expect of them. If there were no agreement about these matters social life would be impossible. Life itself would become chaotic and incomprehensible. For it is partly through interaction with others and through common understandings, that individuals are able to plan and interpret their own thoughts and actions.

Some of these common understandings are explicit, external 'rules' imposed from the outside. However, a great many are simply common assumptions that people make about how things should be done. They may not feel like assumptions or beliefs at all. Rather, they may feel like 'facts of life' which do not change and are not questioned. It is a fact of life that 'Women are like this. Men are like that'; 'This is what women do. This is what men do'. Individuals who live according to these beliefs do NOT feel that they are imposed on them, nor do they feel that they are alien – at least for a good deal of the time. The beliefs become a part of them. That is, they ascribe to themselves the qualities of the group to which they see they belong; they want to do what is expected of them; and they value the socially recognized goals.

When people do this, it is not because they are 'conditioned' or 'brainwashed' or 'conformist' or whatever. It is because, *within a particular social framework*, it is the rational thing to do. It makes sense. So long as society is organized according to a particular set of beliefs, and so long as most people act vaguely in accordance with them, it would be exceedingly difficult to see things in any other way and even more difficult to act differently. For to change such basic ways of looking at things would mean changing the structure of society. It would be particularly difficult for any single individual to contravene the rules, in isolation.

So when we ask an individual woman what women are like, how she sees herself and what she wants, we must look to see how her views make sense for her of the particular social world in which she lives. What one wants depends in part on what looks possible.

One of the things that prevents women from seeing new

14

possibilities is that many of the basic assumptions that people make about women's roles are not explicitly verbalized. Some are of course. For example, there is a much publicized debate as to whether mothers should work, and how old their children should be when they do. Some questions, on the other hand, are never asked even by research workers. Where is the question-naire which asks whether it is right for fathers of young children to work, or whether they should have shorter working hours to allow them time to take half-shares in housework and childcare? The answers to questions about what women 'ought' to do, depend partly on assumptions which are not stated.

One might think that when assumptions are universally shared they are also likely to be made explicit. But Bott, for example, in her study of couples in *Family and Social Network* (1957), suggests that although there were enormous differences between couples in what they believed family roles should be, there were certain norms which were taken for granted and not explicitly stated in so many words.

'All couples took it for granted that there should be a basic division of labour between husband and wife in which the husband was primarily responsible for supporting the family financially and the wife was primarily responsible for looking after the children and seeing that housework and cooking were done. The world would be upside down if the woman went out to work and the husband stayed home to care for the house and children.' (Bott 1957:197)

It may be very difficult in practice to flout norms which are spoken, but it is much more difficult even to question norms which are not articulated at all.

Beliefs about sex roles past and present

What goes without saying in one culture may look more than bizarre to another. In this book we limit ourselves to looking at research on modern western societies. It is just as well to re-member that this *is* a limitation: anthropologists are begin-ning to look at the important question of why it is that in one

15

society women have certain roles and are seen in a particular way – while in another it is quite different. Their findings may eventually help us to interpret present assumptions. (For further reading on this see Rosaldo and Lamphere 1974; Chodorow 1971; Chodorow 1974.)

Some knowledge of the way sex roles have developed historically within our own culture is also important. Many people who accept that sex roles have actually changed, see this as a simple question of progress: in the old days, so the story goes, women were unfairly treated whereas now they are gaining equality and respect. The reality is not so simple. There is a great deal of disagreement among sociologists and historians about just how and why sex roles have come to be as they are now. Much of the research remains to be done. Again, a full discussion of this is beyond the scope of the present book. But a brief look at some of the changes in the recent past may help us to see present-day assumptions more clearly, in contrast, and to understand better what may be influencing women and men today. (Those interested in following this up could start by reading Zeretsky (1976) and Oakley (1974b). We have drawn heavily from these works in the following paragraphs.)

In pre-capitalist societies, such as feudal England, and in the early stages of capitalism, work and family life overlapped a good deal. The household was a basic unit of production. In other words the home was a place of work. Roles were usually segregated by sex and age. But men, women, and children all took part in the production of goods for exchange and for sale, as well as for immediate consumption by the family. There was no clear distinction between the role of worker and the role of family member. So it is unlikely that a woman was able to think of herself as 'housewife' or 'mother' *instead of* 'worker' since the two were not separate. Thus the *kinds* of conflicts and arguments that we have today about women's roles would not have arisen.

In pre-industrial Britain, then, women played an important part in production. Some achieved a good deal of independence (Oakley 1974b). We are not arguing that, overall, women's lives were easier than after industrialization. Many worked for long hours and for little reward, and with very little control over their lives. But the form of their oppression was different.

Capitalist production and industrialization, together, radically changed the nature of work and family life, and the relationship between the two. Productive work moved from the home to the factory where workers sold their labour power in exchange for money. A new separation developed between the sphere of family life and the sphere of productive work. This does not mean that women did not do paid work. Women and children were at first a ready source of cheap labour for factories and farms.

When increasing industrialization brought rising unemployment and lower wages, many women were driven out of employment and into a new kind of dependency. Others were forced to work for low wages to supplement the incomes of their husbands.

The crucial change was that work came to be defined as labour power which could be sold for a wage which, in turn, could buy other commodities necessary for the worker and HIS family. Work done in the home was increasingly restricted to the service and maintenance of the worker and producing children. And it was no longer seen as 'real' work. Long, hard, and often unpleasant but necessary domestic work could not be sold directly for a wage and so was, in a sense, devalued. At the same time, the family became more and more a private world to which people withdrew.

With this work–family separation came a new kind of division of roles between the sexes. Man became the 'breadwinner' and woman the dependent 'homemaker' responsible for domestic work, children, and private personal life. This ideology seems to have taken a long time to become generally accepted. Apart from a small number of upper-class women, the new middle-classes adopted it first. For them, an idle wife was a living, breathing proof that a man was doing well in the world. Working-class women were usually forced to work outside the home. Apparently it was only during the second half of the nineteenth century that the idea that women ought not to be at work really took hold among the working classes.

However, being at home, as housewife and mother purely, now had a new meaning. For it meant being non-productive, economically dependent, and isolated and apart from the society.

To sum up, then, women always have worked, both inside and outside the home. But working life itself has changed and with it the form of family life, sex-role divisions, and stereotypes.

During this century, attitudes to women taking paid work have fluctuated considerably. For example, during the war, women were needed in the labour force to do the jobs that men were not there to do. It was suddenly in the interests of the state and industry to encourage married women with children to work. To make it easier for them to do so, crêches and nurseries were provided in many places. After the war, many women wished to keep their jobs, but were expected to make way for the returning men. So the facilities disappeared. Many factories also stopped arranging their shifts to suit women (Banner 1974; Adam 1975).

There was an upsurge of feeling against women working. Women were exhorted by 'experts' to stay at home with their children, lest they grew up disturbed and deprived. But women who nevertheless worked, from necessity or choice, had to combine being mother, housewife, and paid worker, in the most difficult conditions. There were few proper nurseries; they had no help in the house from their men and working hours were often awkward for a mother. In such conditions, some children were inevitably neglected and the prophecies of 'experts' became self-fulfilling. But it is mothers and not governments, industry, or fathers who are blamed for the neglect. In the short term, it is in the interests of governments and industry that women should carry the blame, since providing nurseries, or reorganizing jobs, is expensive. Only when there is a demand for women's labour as, for example, in wartime, does 'woman as worker' come to be seen as desirable and find its way into official ideology and practice.

Nonetheless, the numbers of women in paid work dropped only temporarily. Overall, they have been on the increase throughout the century and especially during and after World War II. In Britain in 1961, around 30 per cent of married women were working (Fogarty, Rapoport and Rapoport 1971). Very many more single women were working, of course. In the

United States in 1960, almost 20 per cent of mothers of pre-school children were in the labour force (Nye and Hoffman 1963a). In 1971, half of all American women between the ages of sixteen and sixty-five years, and half of all British women were classed as part of the labour force (Draeger 1972; Cullen 1972).

Another way in which the lives of women and men have changed in the Western world in this century, is in the control of fertility and childbearing. The drop in infant mortality made it unnecessary to produce so many children. This, together with the greater availability and efficiency of contraception, made it possible for women to avoid becoming pregnant repeatedly throughout their fertile years. Another important change has been the increase in life expectation.

Some present-day assumptions about women – explicit and implicit

Study after study has reported that the overwhelming majority of girls and women expect and wish to get married and have children. They formulate this intention earlier and in greater numbers than boys and men, and usually well before they have views on the possible work they may do. In fact, it is rather misleading to speak of marriage as an intention since it does not seem to occur to most women that there is an option. Marriage and childbearing are assumed to be an essential part of one's identity as a woman. Even couples who ultimately have no children seem to arrive at this by a gradual process, rather than by a conscious decision at any point in time. Childbearing is repeatedly postponed in favour of other activities, until finally it is abandoned altogether (Veevers 1973).

The assumption that a woman's primary identity is that of 'homemaker' or 'housewife' assigns to her not one, but three roles : wife, houseworker, and childrearer. A common belief is that these roles are 'naturally' and inextricably linked, and that they are 'naturally' performed by one person. In fact, there is no necessary connection; it is logically possible for the various roles to be performed by different people, and with the exception of giving birth, those other people need not be women.

Whether this would be desirable or not is a separate issue. The point here is that the linking of roles appears to be a fact of life, but actually reflects a particular set of institutions and beliefs.

Moreover, the work that women do in the home because they are women (washing, cleaning, sewing, preparing food, looking after children, waiting for the gasman, caring for the sick, shopping, and so on and so forth) is not seen for what it is. That is, socially productive and essential work which someone would have to be paid to do if women did not do it for free. Yet men's performance of their paid work role is made possible by the socially necessary work performed by women at home.

Oakley (1974a; 1974b) pointed out that some aspects of women's activities have received a great deal of attention from sociologists, while one has been virtually ignored – the actual work involved in running a home. 'By far the largest segment of sociological literature concerning women is focused on their roles as wives, mothers, and housewives – but not on the housewife's role as *houseworker*' (Oakley 1974b : 17).

Oakley also suggests that the characteristic features of the housewife's role in modern industrialized society are : (1) its exclusive allocation to women, rather than to adults of both sexes; (2) its association with economic dependence, i.e. with the dependent role of the woman in modern marriage; (3) its *status as non-work* – or its opposition to 'real' or economically productive work; and (4) its *primacy*, i.e. its priority over other roles.

The third point is particularly important. Housework is not seen as 'real' work because there is no end product for which the woman is paid. Yet various studies in Europe and the United States in recent years suggest that women spend on average around seventy hours a week doing housework (Oakley 1974a). Not only is housework not seen as real work, it differs from other work by being concealed. Because, 'it is private, it is self-defined and its outlines are blurred by its integration in a whole complex of domestic, family-based roles which define the situation of women as well as the situation of the housewife' (Oakley 1974a : 6).

Just as there is no question as to whether most women will become wives and mothers, so there is no debate as to whether women should be houseworkers (and conversely, no serious discussion of whether men should work). Women become houseworkers by virtue of getting married and having children. Insofar as the matter of housework does get an airing, it is in terms of whether, and how much, men should 'help'. The rare couples who genuinely attempt to share housework responsibilities equally, run into considerable practical difficulties and a great deal of opposition.

Rossi (1972) has suggested that people are more ready to admit ambivalence about a role when it is optional. As marriage is not seen by society as an optional role for women, they may be less willing to admit to themselves, as well as to researchers, a lack of desire to become wives and mothers. On the other hand, it is more acceptable to admit ambivalence concerning the optional role of paid work.

Thus, when women are asked for their views on whether women should work outside the home, they may assume that the question is whether women should be workers before they marry or whether they should be workers as well as being wives and mothers. Paid work is an additional role. Very rarely do they see it as an alternative identity.

Some problems with these assumptions

The image of woman as wife and mother only and man as breadwinner is a myth. As an account of what is actually happening, it is, and always has been, incomplete, inaccurate, and often downright wrong. At the present time, large numbers of women, including mothers, are doing what they are not supposed to be doing – they are at work, either from necessity or choice. Many are sole supporters of their families.

Nonetheless, the myth is a powerful one. Most people still think that the debate concerning women's roles is mainly about work roles. For many, the question of whether women should work now sounds 'old hat'. It has generally been elaborated and now questions concern more the circumstances in which women should work, the kind of work role they should have and so forth. But perceptions of women's role in the work force influence, and are influenced by, perceptions of their other roles. It is because women are expected to be primarily responsible for housework and childrearing, and to have that as their main function in life, that they are limited in their work role. It also leads to their being vulnerable to exploitation as workers.

A married woman must take what work she can get. She must find a job wherever her husband's work takes him – and it must fit in with housework and children. Her wage is seen as supplementing her husband's, not supporting herself and her family. Many women accept this definition of their work. They put up with lower wages than men, and are less likely to join trade unions or defend their jobs and incomes. In Britain and the United States women still receive less training, are concentrated in low-paying occupations, often receive less pay than men for comparable work, and are less likely to reach higher grades and salaries in their jobs. They can be taken on when there is a demand for labour and laid off easily during recessions, since they are not seen as breadwinners and do not see themselves that way.

The complicated and exhausting business of juggling the roles of paid work outside the home and unpaid housework, also falls mainly on the woman. Government help is almost negligible. In 1971, in Britain more than half of all adult working women had children under sixteen years of age and 20 per cent of these had children under five. Yet there were nursery school places for only around 24,000 children, though the total number of children in this age group was around two and half million (Cullen 1972). Moreover, even in families in which the mother is working, the major part of the housework is done by the wife. But the very problems women face at work and in combining the two roles, help maintain a situation in which most women make marriage and family their main or exclusive role.

Yet the wife-and-mother image is also an inaccurate picture of even the most devoted homemaker. Lopata (1971) suggests that in the course of a life-time, a housewife goes through several major changes in the nature of her roles. Early in the marriage she may have a close relationship with her husband, perhaps a job and many activities and friendships outside the home. As a a young mother she is practically and psychologically confined by her small children and has to modify her personality, her interests, and her behaviour. Gradually, as the children grow older, they need her less and less. When they leave home she loses what is often seen as her main role in life. At this point, many women seize the opportunity to pursue their own interests, or become involved in work or community activities; others are at a loss.

> 'The average American woman now lives to age 74 and has her last child in her late twenties; thus, by the time the woman is 33 or so, her children all have more important things to do with their daytime hours than spend them entertaining an adult woman who has nothing better to do during the second half of her life-span.'
>
> (Bem and Bem 1970:94)

Another problem with the myth is that it ignores class and subcultural differences in sex-role norms and practical circumstances. The meanings of marriage and singlehood, motherhood and childlessness, working and not working, are not the same for all women. The concrete physical demands placed on women by the various roles, and the effects that the roles have on each other, vary enormously. Thus, for example, the effects of work for a wife depend among other things on the kind of work she can get, what she is paid, and whether there are nurseries for the children. And the meaning of motherhood depends partly on the kinds of relationships a woman has outside her marriage with parents, other relatives, and friends in the local community and so on.

Options perceived and available

When we look at some of the research studies which attempt to find out what women think the roles of women are and should be, the points made above have to be borne in mind. What women want and what they think ought to happen, are not necessarily the same. Both may depend in part on what the options are and, more importantly, *what women perceive them to be*. For example, take a woman who works out of necessity at a physically tiring, boring, and low-paid job, who is forced to

23

leave her children with unsatisfactory childminders, and who must find time to do housework and childcare unaided. This woman might reasonably conclude that the world would be a better place if women did not have to work. For that is the option most nearly within her grasp, even if unattainable. On the other hand, take a young middle-class woman, who has been discouraged from ambition because she is a woman. She knows that her social status and relationships depend on her performance as a wife and mother and she is making sense of the world as she knows it if she makes that her main goal. But what of the highly educated and trained woman who can command an interesting and well-paid job? She can pay for private nursery schools and help with the housework, and can perhaps find a husband with egalitarian views as well. Is it not more likely that she will decide that women should make use of their talents and 'fulfil themselves' at work? The real and the perceived options are quite different in these three examples. For any of the women to imagine very different options would involve a revolutionary change both in the way they see themselves and society, as well as in the organization of that society.

As a society, we construct the social world according to our interests and beliefs; and as individuals we construct our beliefs to make sense of our own particular experiences of the world. So shared beliefs and experiences support each other – at least for a good deal of the time. Sex-role norms do not exist only inside people's heads. They influence people's behaviour. We are constantly giving each other evidence to support our beliefs.

The other side of the coin is that when events do not conform to expectation they are often simply ignored. And if an individual woman does decide that the roles laid down for her are in other people's interests but not her own, it can be very difficult for her to change her situation by herself. She does not have the power to change institutions single-handed.

Having set the framework within which men and women operate, we can now look at some of the evidence showing what those shared beliefs are, what is considered to be the appropriate behaviour for each sex and what influences these – for better or for worse.

TWO

Women on the woman's place

What *should* women do with their lives? What roles *should* they take on? It is very easy to show that most people think that a woman's place in the world should be broadly different from a man's – even if they disagree on how different it should be. Several surveys of opinions on this matter have in fact been carried out in Europe and the United States. In the main, people have been asked to make broad generalizations. Should women have the same opportunities as men in education and work? Should women work? Should mothers work? Or should they concentrate on being mothers? Which roles should they put first in life? Should husbands help with the housework? And so on.

Such surveys have an uncanny habit of telling us what we already know. If the main object of the exercise is to find out that men are supposed to be breadwinners and women wives and mothers, then we hardly need a survey. But the real interest here is in what lies behind the answers. Why is it that people choose certain values? What implications do their values have for them? Some hypotheses about this come from finding out what sort of people have a particular view. How do they differ – in their experiences, their hopes and prospects, or in their vested interests – from other people holding contrasting opinions?

For practical reasons much of the information needed to answer these kinds of questions is missing from large-scale surveys. Certain broad and crude relationships can be looked at however. First, we can find out whether women agree with men about what they should be doing. This is important since a good many decisions affecting women are made by men. Second, we can ask whether practical circumstances make any difference to a woman's views – being married, being a mother, or having a job, and the type of job and level of income. Third, we can look at the influence of a woman's background – education and class, for instance, and the kind of community she comes from. We can also get some idea of the relationship between values on different issues. Does a person who approves of mothers working also approve of husbands doing housework, for example?

A word of caution is needed here: surveys can be immensely misleading. Any politician knows that the results of opinion polls are very much influenced by the way a question is put to people. And simple questions generate simple answers. Some questions are never asked at all, because of the researchers' own biases. Also, we cannot assume that just because everyone was asked the same question, the question meant the same thing to all of them. For example, take the question of whether women should work. A mother of two toddlers and a baby who answers this, may have in mind other women in the same position. It is easy for her to forget that a woman can be a mother thirty years after her children have grown up, and that some wives have no children, and some mothers no husbands. A forty-five-year-old divorcee would have a different frame of reference. A man might say that he approves of women working, but mean by this only young unmarried women and mothers of grown children, and only as long as her work does not interfere with his supper. Or he might mean that her work is good for her and that he would support her in any way possible.

When should a woman have a paid job?

The central issue for most people is whether *wives* should work.

(a) *America*. Nye (1974c) concerned himself specifically with this. He asked a sample of women and men in the State of Washington this question: 'There has also been a trend toward more women being employed outside the home than in the past. Do you think this trend toward more women working is desirable or undesirable?' (Nye 1974c:12).

Table 1 Attitudes towards the gainful employment of married women.

	% favourable responses	% unfavourable responses	% undecided
males, all ages	49	42	9
females, all ages	43	44	13
males, under 35	61	31	8
females, under 35	63	28	8

(Source: Nye 1974c:12)

As can be seen from *Table 1*, among men and women of all ages attitudes are divided roughly equally for and against. But in the younger age group a majority of both women and men favour work for married women. We need to be careful about what this actually means. The question is being asked in its most general form. There is no mention of how much work, what type of work, whether women with children of any age should work, or what concessions the husband should make to the wife's work role. The experience of other studies is that when the question is put in a more precise way, fewer people say they favour women working. This lack of precision may also explain why there is not the difference of opinion often found between the sexes.

Hoffman (1974b) reviewing the literature on American studies of attitudes to maternal exployment, finds that a number of studies show that working mothers are more likely to approve of work and to say that their husbands do too. One study also found that among white women, the more educated the woman, the more likely she was to be in favour of work for mothers of school age children. Women with college education were twice as likely to approve, when compared with less educated women. Among black women, education made no consistent difference. Black women with very limited education, as well as college-educated black women, approved of working mothers more than white women did.

(b) *France*. In France, a survey carried out by the Groupe d'Ethnologie Sociale (Chombart de Lauwe 1962) investigated sex-role norms held by parents at three different income levels. Sixty lower-income couples and sixty middle-income couples, living in Paris and its suburbs were interviewed. Only couples with children were selected. Husband and wife were interviewed separately. In response to the very general question 'Do you approve of women being employed in regular jobs?' only about 20 per cent of the men in either group said they did. The women saw things differently; about half of the lower income women and 65 per cent of the middle-income women approved. Few people objected to work for single women or widows.

When it came to the specific question of whether married women with no children should work, women and men differed again. Almost all the women were in favour, whereas only just over half the lower-income and two-thirds of the middle-income husbands were. On the whole, both men and women disapproved of work for mothers with young children. Rather more of the women than the men favoured work for mothers of school age children, 25 per cent and 16·7 per cent respectively in the lower-income group and 30 per cent and 20 per cent respectively in the middle-income group.

What one approves of is not necessarily the same as one's preference. When the women were asked what they would *prefer* to do, about three-quarters of the lower-income women said they would prefer not to work. Their attitudes were not affected by whether or not they were actually working. By contrast, more of the middle-income group liked what they were doing. Only one quarter of the middle-income mothers who were working would have liked to give it up; and more than half of those who were not working preferred it that way.

In the debate about working mothers, the woman's own interests (as opposed to the needs of husband and children) are often given little importance. It is interesting that in this sample just under a third of middle-income women and a quarter of lower-income women thought that paid work is good 'for the woman herself'; fewer men thought so.

Thus from this study, we have two general conclusions. One is that these women are consistently more approving than the men, of women being employed. This is true even among lower-income women. However, middle-income women are more in favour than the lower-income women. This may be partly because in families with higher incomes the women have more choice in the work they can do. They also have more means available with which to resolve the conflicting demands of the two roles. Housework aids and help with childcare may make a crucial difference, as may a less physically demanding job. Middle-income husbands tend to be somewhat more egalitarian, which may also help.

(c) *Poland*. A similar study in Poland, reported by Piotrowski (1962) is interesting since some degree of sex-role equality has been supported by official ideology and legislation for a longer period in Socialist countries. Attitudes to women's roles, and especially work outside the home were compared in three different working-class groups. The interviews were of 100 families in Warsaw, in which the husband was a metal worker, 103 families in Lodz, in which the husbands were textile workers, and 172 families in Silesia, in which the husbands were miners. The groups varied both in the work available to the women and in the local traditions concerning women's work. In Warsaw women have ample and varied opportunities for employment; in Lodz, the employment of women is said to be regarded as normal and traditional with wide opportunities for employment, and low men's wages producing greater pressure for women to go out and earn money; the Silesian mining families are said to be homogeneous and isolated communities, in which women have few opportunities for work, men's wages are high, and the tradition is strongly against women working.

In Warsaw and Lodz, there are more women wanting to work outside the home than there are husbands wanting them to work. Unlike the previous studies, these women were asked their personal wishes, rather than their views on women's roles in general. In passing, we may note that the views of the husbands as to whether women should work, vary by group as expected. In Warsaw and Lodz the majority favour equal rights and pay for women and think that women with no children should work. The Silesian husbands are against work even for childless women. All the husbands are against work for mothers of young children. An interesting point is that the husbands tend to have different preferences for their *own* wives. They are more likely to prefer that their own wives do not work.

Of the women's feelings on the work they do, Piotrowski comments that it seems that most of the wives in employment want to give it up, while most of those who do not work would like to! This may say more than that the grass is greener ... On the whole, the Warsaw and Lodz families are relatively poor. The decision about whether to work is probably made from necessity and not preference. The disagreement between the workers and non-workers, is especially strong in Lodz, where the husbands' incomes are low, and women who can make arrangements for the children must be under strong pressure to work, regardless of whether they wish to work or like the work that they do. Also, being poor makes housework more unpleasant and a wage more attractive; but it also makes combining a job with housework and looking after children more difficult.

This is an important point to bear in mind. Poorer working-class women have very little choice as to whether they work or not; insofar as they do have a choice, both the available alternatives may be bad ones.

Nonetheless, the finding is again that more women than men favour women's employment.

(d) *Norway.* In Norway, Holter (1970) conducted a series of studies which provide some of the most extensive data available on sex-role norms for a wide range of activities (education, political life, occupational life, and family life) in a variety of social groups. In one study, non-supervisory employees, 591 blue-collar workers and 397 white-collar workers were drawn from a number of firms in Oslo. Each filled in an extensive questionnaire which covered, among other things, attitudes to sex-role divisions in activity, work, and work behaviour.

In a second study, three groups of Norwegian housewives were compared. Fifty were not in paid work and were from a stable rural community; fifty were staying at home, and fifty held jobs outside the home and came from an urban indus-trialized community in Eastern Norway. All the women had husbands whose incomes were average for the community, were thirty to forty years of age and had children below fifteen-years-old. They were interviewed personally and asked to com-plete a brief questionnaire. Among other questions, they were asked for their views on the division of labour within and out-side the home.

A third survey was of ex-students who had passed the quali-fication for university entrance in Norway twenty-five years previously. Over 2,000 ex-students were approached and, of these, 75 per cent completed a questionnaire which included eight questions on sex-role differentiation.

Holter made some interesting comparisons between the views on women's work and sex roles, held by the different social groups. For instance, the views of the Oslo employees on women's employment are given in *Table 2* below. Note that the Table includes the data for both sexes.

At first sight, there appears to be some inconsistency in the answers. When asked about equal opportunities at work, almost three-quarters of the respondents seem to accept the principle. Yet half say that women should be at home and not at work at all. Some of them must be in some doubt about what women should be doing. Or perhaps they think that equal opportunities are for spinsters and widows. But when beliefs and customs are changing, people can hold conflicting views at the same time, although a person's tolerance of this is, of course, limited.

There are several other interesting findings from this series of studies. For instance, it is the question of division of work (whether women should stick to the home and whether men should do housework) that distinguishes most strongly between the sexes. On other issues (education, political activity, and who

Table 2 Percentage responses of Oslo employers to three questions.

item	agree %	uncertain %	disagree %	N/A %	total %
'Women ought to stick to the care of home and children'	53	15	24	8	100
'Women ought to get as many chances as men for advancement in occupational life'	73	11	7	9	100
'Women ought not to have managing or leading positions in occupational life'	16	23	51	10	100

(Source: Holter 1970:57)

makes decisions in the home and so on) there is less disagreement between men and women. Although many people of both sexes did think that men's and women's roles should be very different, women were significantly more likely to favour employment for women. This was so among both the Oslo employees and the ex-students. Less than a third of women ex-students as compared with half the men ex-students would 'prefer women to be mothers and housewives'. But 24 per cent of the women ex-students and only 7 per cent of the men agreed with the much more extreme statement that they would 'prefer a new division of work in the family and occupational life' (Holter 1970:71).

Did people who believed in similar roles for the two sexes in one area, such as work, also tend to favour similar roles in other areas, such as education or housework? Holter found that they did to some extent, though by no means consistently. (Many people who accept equal education balk at the idea of equality in housework or paid work.) She compiled what she calls an 'index of traditionalism' from the data on attitudes to education, political life, and family life. By traditionalism she meant holding the view that men and women should have generally very different roles. The contrasting view she calls 'egalitarianism', this being the idea that the two sexes should be treated similarly.

She found that egalitarianism correlated with education. Better educated people were more likely to favour similar roles. The relationship was stronger among women than among men. But it held true for married and unmarried, for working and non-working wives, for husbands with working wives, and for husbands with non-working wives.

Holter suggests a number of reasons for this relationship. A selection process may operate, so that women with egalitarian views are more likely to seek higher education. Education may confront students with 'humanistic' and 'democratic' values, as well as make them examine traditional beliefs not supported by scientific evidence. Or:

'Higher education tends to de-emphasise criteria which buttress a traditional division of labor, such as physical strength and emotional dispositions and at the same time favours qualities, such as intellectual capacities, which are more equally bestowed on men and women.'

(Holter 1970:64)

At school and university, students see that women do as well as men. However, is it not quite likely that better educated women will tend to get more attractive jobs, better pay, and prospects? So they have more means for dealing with the practical conflicts between work and family roles.

Interestingly, the type of job a woman had (blue-collar versus white-collar) made no difference to the likelihood of her holding egalitarian views, except insofar as it was associated with education. But this might be because only a small number of different kinds of jobs were sampled, as Holter points out.

When she compared the two sexes for egalitarianism, Holter found again that the women were more frequently egalitarian than the men. This tendency was found in all age groups,

33

among blue-collar and white-collar employees, and in groups with similar levels of education and with similar backgrounds. She infers that women are generally more dissatisfied than men with present sex-role norms because, in general in the present system, men have more prestige and power and women more strains and burdens. Women have less access to goals which men and women are taught to value (see Merton 1968).

This finding is particularly interesting since a common criticism of 'feminists' is that they are a small and non-representative group of (educated) middle-class women who want to impose their views on the mass of happy housewives. Many housewives and many working women may, indeed, be happy, and may be traditional. But there are many signs of conflict and dissent. We would suggest that people do not usually begin to express discontent until they can see the glimmerings of an attainable alternative. This may be one reason why most discontent is heard from educated women.

Holter points out that comparison of her data with data for adolescents (Rommetveit 1954; Brun-Gulbrandsen 1958) suggests that the disagreement between adult men and women is greater than for adolescents, with adolescent girls (and young women) being more traditional. She suggests that advantages accorded the two sexes, are distributed more equally in childhood and adolescence than in adulthood (see Lynn 1959), and that 'women discover that the disadvantages associated with their sex roles increase as they grow older' (Holter 1970:72).

Finally Holter finds that wives who work outside the home have more egalitarian attitudes than other women. It seems that this is more likely to be because egalitarian women seek paid work, rather than because paid work makes women egalitarian, since the single women she interviewed, who presumably work from necessity, are not so egalitarian.

(e) *Finland.* Haavio-Mannila (1972) conducted a survey in Finland of views on sex roles among (a) residents of Helsinki, the capital, (b) women in two small towns and (c) five rural communities. A total of about 1,000 people were interviewed aged between fifteen and sixty-five years. The survey took place in 1966. In 1970, some of the same items were included in a

Gallup Poll of over 1,000 Finns, and Haavio-Mannila compared these responses with those from the earlier survey to see in what ways attitudes had changed.

The results were in many ways similar to those of the surveys already discussed. As in the French and Norwegian studies, Finnish women in all groups were more egalitarian as regards sex roles than were the men. Not surprisingly, married employed women were the most often in favour of women working and of men helping with the housework, whereas non-working wives were the least in favour of women working. In all but one of the Finnish samples, education was once again related with attitudes to women's employment, with more educated people being in favour.

Did attitudes change between 1966 and 1970? It seems that they did to a considerable extent. There was much more widespread egalitarianism. However, Haavio-Mannila is doubtful as to how far the differences in replies were really due to fundamental changes in beliefs and behaviour and how far they just reflected lip-service to views for which there had been a good deal of propaganda.

The role of the houseworker

The word 'houseworker' is used because we want to focus on the work of running a house, as distinct from all the many activities covered by the work 'housewife'.

Holter (1970) in her Norwegian studies, asked both women and men about housework. Almost half of the Oslo employees thought that men should 'leave housework to the housewife', and one third disagreed with this view. Of the housewives from small towns, half thought men should not do housework, and 41 per cent that they should. Interestingly, a large majority in all groups thought that 'boys ought to learn domestic work (housework) as much as girls'.

Does this mean that the people who say that men should do some housework actually believe that housework is not in some special way a 'woman's role'? That men should do a significant part of it, or even take equal shares? Not really. The questions are vaguely phrased. So anyone who thought that a husband should from time to time 'help the wife' with the washing up, or mend the lawn-mower, would be included in the group who do not think that men should leave domestic work to women. And people who thought that boys should know how to do domestic work need not necessarily have thought that men should actually do any, if there were a woman around. Studies which look at what men and women actually do as housework, usually find that by far the greater part is done by the wife, even when she has a strong career committment (Fogarty, Rapoport, and Rapoport 1971). Oakley (1974b) points out that research workers who claim that families are becoming more 'symmetrical' in their division of work, have usually taken a very low level of participation in housework by the husband as evidence of role sharing.

Haavio-Mannila, in the Finnish survey just described, also found that a substantial percentage of people were in favour of men doing some housework (see *Table 3*). But the women were

Table 3 Percentage responses from men and women in urban and rural areas in Finland, agreeing that men should do some housework.

	1966		1970	
	Helsinki %	Rural %	Helsinki %	Rural %
men	21	36	57	48
women	38	50	78	79

(Source: Haario-Mannila 1972:98 and 101)

more likely to think that men should do some housework, than the men were to think that they should. In 1966, 38 per cent of the women in the Helsinki sample, as compared with 21 per cent of the men and 50 per cent of the women in rural areas, as compared with 36 per cent of these men, did *not* think that 'in general men should leave the household tasks to the women'. Eighty-one per cent of the husbands, as compared with only 48 per cent of the wives, were 'very satisfied' with the amount of housework done by the spouse.

By 1970, there had been some change in attitudes, in that

nearly 80 per cent of the women, and around half the men, over-all, now thought that men should not leave household tasks to women entirely.

As in the Norwegian study, these figures do not tell us any-thing about the amount of housework the respondents thought men should do, or how much they did in practice. Haavio-Mannila comments that the discrepancy between the sexes probably reflects a sense of injustice on the part of the women, many of whom work from necessity and have to manage two jobs – one inside and one outside the home.

Sometimes, however, it is found that women are actually more resistant than men to the idea of men doing housework (see, for example, Chombart de Lauwe 1962). Perhaps a woman who sees being a homemaker as her main purpose in life, fears that this purpose will be taken away? Allowing the man to do housework threatens her identity – for it means that the man might take over the role. If such a woman is no longer able to see herself as a housewife, how does she know who she is?

The 'traditional' image: mother, wife, and housewife

A large number of studies have shown that patterns of be-haviour within families, the activities and roles of husband and wife, and relationships with other kin and neighbours, vary a good deal between classes, and from one community to an-other (see, for example, Bott 1957; Toomey 1971; Bahr 1974; Nye 1974a; Hobart 1973; Wilmott and Young 1967; Gavron 1975). Not all these studies have actually asked the women what they thought women's roles should be, but we can expect varia-tion in attitudes as well as in behaviour.

The strength of the (supposedly) 'traditional' image of woman as primarily mother, wife, and homemaker, at least in one section of the population, is shown by the American study of Lopata (1971). She was interested in 'women who perform the social role of housewife' and live in urban areas of the United States. Her definition of a housewife is 'a woman who is re-sponsible for running her home', whether she does the work her-self or pays someone else to do it for her. The study focuses on women who are involved in the role and mainly at the stage in

life when they have husbands and growing children. She conducted interviews with 268 surburban housewives, 200 urban
non-working housewives, and 100 working wives (who were
also, of course, housewives).

Nearly all the women had worked at some time in their
lives. Of those not working at the time of the study, nearly half
had no intention of working in the future. Thus, it is in part a
study of women who had chosen, or accepted, the 'housewife' role, and allows some comparison with women who were
also in paid work. The women were asked, 'What are the most
important roles of a woman, in order of importance?' The per-

Table 4 Percentage of women naming different roles as being
of importance.

role	suburban housewives %	urban housewives %	working women %	total %
mother	80	83	41	74
wife	57	67	64	71
housewife	60	64	37	58
family, care of	9	-9	1	8
community member, society	26	17	14	21
friend, neighbour	4	3	7	4
daughter, other relative	0	3	1	1
self, duties towards	25	6	5	8
no. of respondents	268	200	100	568

(Source: Lopata 1971:48)

centages of women naming the different roles in answer to the
question are given in *Table 4* above.

Lopata was impressed by the fact that 'four-fifths of our 568
interviewees, one hundred of whom are currently working, do
not feel the importance of female participation in the life of the
society sufficiently to remember such obligations in answers to
open-ended questions' (Lopata 1971). The working women
were, in fact, even less likely to mention roles outside the home
than were the non-working women. Nor did most of the replies
distinguish between women at different ages, with or without
children, or with children of different ages. Perhaps the women
assumed that the questions referred to women like themselves,

mainly at the stage of life when the family is increasing and the children are growing and time-consuming? The curious part, however, as Lopata points out, is that very many of these women were in fact, currently involved in roles outside the home, in community activities, as friends and neighbours and some were working. They presumably had additional evidence around them that it is difficult for a woman to make being a mother the central or exclusive role for the whole of her life. It seems possible that cultural norms influence perceptions. On the one hand, the changing roles that women can have, in the full course of their lives, may be forgotten, and on the other, activities in which they are highly involved in practice, are not seen as important merely because they are not supposed to be important.

The various roles that women can have, within the family, were not of equal importance. Lopata asked them to rank various roles. The roles of 'wife' and 'mother' were ranked of most importance by a long way. What is interesting is that it was the roles within the immediate family that were most valued. Relationships with parents or other kin came much lower on the list.

When they were asked what were the most important satisfactions of the 'homemaker' role, 38 per cent mentioned children, and only 9 per cent mentioned the husband or a happy marriage. It looks as if motherhood is a more socially valued role than wifehood.

A rather ominous finding was their views on the importance of the role of grandmother. Very few indeed ranked the role of grandmother high in importance for a woman, and it was the role most frequently ranked last. Since the majority did not see roles outside the family as important, one is left with the impression that a woman's life is a descent from a highly valued role, the role of mother, to one that has only marginal significance.

Some comments

What conclusions can we draw from all this? As expected, there are some differences and also certain broad similarities between various Western countries in attitudes to sex roles. Most people think it right and proper that women should be wives and mothers, and put these roles first in their lives. The basic assumptions are that marriage, motherhood, and home-making go together, that they are a woman's job, and that anything else a woman does comes second. It must not interfere with the family. So if she has small children she must not work, and even if she works full time she should still do the bulk of the housework, and so on. The wife-and-mother image is so strong that most people and most researchers forget to take into account the single, the childless, widows, and women whose children have grown up. How often has anyone been asked what kinds of roles a grandmother should have?

This we already knew. What might surprise more people is the extent of the disagreement between women and men. Again and again we find that more women than men approve of women having paid jobs. And not only middle-class or better educated women, contrary to one popular myth. Moreover, more women than men think men should do more housework.

There are certain differences between women too. Highly educated women more often think that women should work, and generally favour more similar roles for the two sexes. Working mothers more often approve of working mothers. The effects of type of occupation and income are less clear.

Why the differences between women and men? And among women themselves? It is not surprising that women and men disagree about sex roles: their circumstances are different and the personal and practical implications of organizing sex roles in a particular way, are obviously very different for the two sexes. (For example, when sex roles are more similar men have to be more involved in housework and childcare and women less so.) Similar considerations apply to people in different social groups. But what implications do these people themselves see? To find out more about that we need to look at a different kind of research.

THREE

Women on women's personalities

If most people believe that women and men not only do have, but also should have, different roles and goals in everyday life, we might expect that they also see the two sexes as differing in their personal qualities. The view that men should be bread-winners and women, first and foremost, mothers and house-wives, is bolstered by the belief that each sex is somehow especially suited to the role prescribed.

We do not necessarily have to argue about which 'comes first', the ideology about role divisions or the beliefs about sex differences in personality. To a large extent they influence and reinforce each other. On the one hand, it is assumed that women must have certain personal qualities since they are found doing certain things. On the other hand, so the story goes, since women do have those qualities, it is only right and proper that they should have the roles that go with them.

Research has shown over and over again that men and women 'see' characteristic differences in personality between 'men in general' and 'women in general'. (See, for example, Fernberger 1948; McKee and Sherriffs 1957; Broverman *et al.* 1972; Huang 1971.) The precise nature of the supposed differences is not entirely constant from study to study. Just how men and women are thought to differ may vary considerably depending on the particular group studied (see, for example, Huang 1971; Turner and Turner 1974).

There is also some evidence, though less consistently found, that men and women also disagree. Fernberger (1948) and Huang (1971) both found that there was a good deal of agreement between the sexes in how each saw women, but the women were much less unfavourably disposed towards women than were the men. For example, Fernberger notes that twice as many men as women, in his sample, thought that 'Women are more unstable emotionally than men are'. At the same time, most studies find a good deal of overlap in qualities which people ascribe to men and women and to themselves (Bennett and Cohen 1959).

Nonetheless, the repeated finding is that people do tend to have different expectations of the two sexes, and within any subculture, there will be a good deal of consensus as to what those differences are. If this is so, we may ask what the relationship is between beliefs about the nature of women and men 'in general' and peoples' views of themselves in particular. Do women 'see' themselves, individually, as having the personalities which women in general are supposed to have?

Rosenkrantz and his colleagues (1968) set out to investigate this question. Seventy-four men and eighty women (all American college students) were presented with 122 items referring to personal qualities, to be rated on a 7-point scale. These items, which formed the 'Stereotype Questionnaire', were laid out as follows:

1. Not at all aggressive   very aggressive
      1.......2.......3.......4.......5.......6.......7

Each person was instructed to put a mark along each scale according to the extent to which it characterized the average male. The actual instructions were to 'imagine that you are going to meet a person for the first time and the only thing you know about him in advance is that the person is an adult male'.

Having gone through the items for the average male, they were asked to go through them again, this time with the average female in mind. There was then a third run through, and this time each person marked the scale according to the extent to which the item was true of himself or herself. To take account of the fact that doing the male rating first might affect the 'female' ratings that followed, and *vice versa*, half the subjects did the 'male' first, and half 'female'. Both men and women agreed as to what constituted the average male and the average female.

On forty-one of the 122 items, the respondents gave significantly different descriptions for men as compared to women. At the same time, there was 75 per cent or more agreement between respondents of each sex, as to which pole was more descriptive of the average man than of the average woman. Rosenkrantz considered this to be good grounds for terming these items 'stereotypic'. (On forty-eight further items, there were significant differences in the descriptions of men and women, in each sample, but the agreement as to the direction of the differences was less than 75 per cent.)

Looking at the results, it seemed possible that not only were men and women perceived as different, but that they were also differently valued. Of the stereotypic items, more socially desirable characteristics were ascribed to men than to women. Social desirability was measured by asking seventy-three men and forty-eight women who had not taken part in the study, to indicate which pole of the 122 bi-polar concepts they thought represented the more socially desirable characteristic, for the population at large. Twenty-nine of the forty-one stereotypic items had the 'masculine' pole chosen as more socially desirable by a majority.

Thus the typical female comes out as someone who: does not use harsh language; is talkative, tactful, gentle; is aware of the feelings of others; is religious, interested in her own appearance, neat in habits, quiet; has a strong need for security, appreciates art and literature, and expresses tender feelings.

Whereas the typical male is someone who: is aggressive, independent, unemotional, or hides his emotions; is objective, easily influenced, dominant, likes maths and science; is not excitable in a minor crisis; is active, competitive, logical, worldly, skilled in business, direct, knows the ways of the world; is someone whose feelings are not easily hurt; is adventurous, makes decisions easily, never cries, acts as a leader; is self-confident; is not uncomfortable about being aggressive; is ambitious, able to separate feelings from ideas; is not dependent, nor conceited about his appearance; thinks men are superior to women, and talks freely about sex with men (see Stricker 1977).

On the face of it, these are rather odd lists. Some of the items ascribed to each sex seem somewhat inconsistent with each other, and others look so similar as to make it doubtful whether they were really seen as separate characteristics. It would be rash, on the basis of this study alone, to jump to the conclusion that women are really being evaluated as possessing fewer socially desirable qualities than men.

We shall come back to this issue. For the moment, we can say that it looks as if the socially desirable qualities men are seen as having, are different from the socially desirable qualities women are seen as having. The male-valued items could best be described as reflecting competency, whereas the female-valued cluster seemed to reflect qualities of warmth and expressiveness.

Having established that the respondents in this sample did see men and women in general as differing in personality, the same authors looked at self-concepts. They found that the mean self-concept scores of the men were significantly different from the mean self-concept scores of the women, over the forty-one stereotypic items on the questionnaire. The women's self-concepts tended to be more similar to the female stereotype and the men's self concepts to be more similar to the male stereotype. This means that, to some extent, both sexes were seeing themselves as similar to what they thought their own sex in general was like. Men thought they had qualities which are socially desirable for men, and women thought they had qualities which are socially desirable for women.

There is, however, an important qualification to be made. When each woman's concept of herself was compared directly to the stereotypic female, there was a significant difference between the two; and the same applied to the men. The women saw themselves as 'less female' and the men saw themselves as 'less male', than they thought most men, or most women, were. The same sort of thing has been found with stereotypes of other groups. For example, the alcoholic shares others' views of the 'typical' alcoholic but does not see himself in these terms (Hoy 1973). The same applies to stutterers (Fransella 1972).

One way of interpreting these findings, would be that, in fact, both women and men were influenced by popular beliefs about the nature of men and women, but that, at the same time, they did not entirely go along with such beliefs, when applied to themselves. (See Fransella 1977 for an extended discussion of the self/stereotype dichotomy.)

Class, culture, and social position as influences on perceptions of women and men

Different studies have not always found exactly the same characteristics being ascribed to typical men nor to typical women. Some of the differences between studies are no doubt due to differences in method. However, since we have seen (in Chapter 2) that beliefs as to what women's roles should be, vary with culture, education, and class, one would like to know how beliefs about personality fit in with this. One piece of evidence comes from an extension of the Rosenkrantz study.

Broverman and her co-workers (1972) obtained replies to the sex-role questionnaire from 599 men and 383 women, married and single, aged from seventeen to sixty years, with educations ranging from elementary to advanced graduate degree level. All were American. A good deal of consensus was in fact found. On forty-seven of the items, there was agreement between people of different ages, education, and marital status. They all saw men and women as significantly different from each other in these respects. However, on other items, some of the groups disagreed. To understand better why they disagreed, we should need more extensive research.

An illustration of the differences that can be found between cultures, is provided by the study by Huang (1971). She asked a group of Chinese students from Taiwan, and a group of American college students, to complete Rosenkrantz's questionnaire.

45

In each of the two national samples, a group of men rated 'male' characteristics, a separate group of men rated 'female' characteristics, a group of women rated 'male' characteristics, and a separate group of women rated 'female' characteristics.

Among both the American and the Chinese students, significant differences were found between the perceptions of men and women. These were in many ways similar to the findings of Rosenkrantz. But there were also major differences between the cultures in their perceptions. The greatest difference was between the view of women held by the American women and that held by the Chinese women. There were significant differences between these two groups on sixty-two of the possible 122 items. In general, the Chinese women seemed to be presenting a more negative view of themselves.

For example, by comparison with the American women, the Chinese women saw women as: having a poorer sense of humour and a weaker personality; less conscientious and less resourceful; more selfish; giving up more easily; less dominant, less adventurous, less inclined to act as leader; and more timid, more afraid to be different, and less creative.

Some of the differences may have occurred because the Chinese women were being more 'modest', as modesty is a highly valued virtue in this Chinese society. In other words, what the Chinese women said may have been more negative, than what they thought. But there do seem to have been some cultural differences over and above this, since the differences between the views of women, held by women, in the two cultures were much greater than the differences between the views of men held by men.

In both cultures, men and women disagreed in their perceptions of women. But the discrepancy between the sexes was even greater among the Chinese students than among the Americans – Chinese men being more negative about women.

Huang argues that we should expect people in the Chinese culture to see greater differences between men and women. She suggests an explanation along the lines described by Barry, Bacon, and Child (1957). They thought that in a nuclear family – consisting of the two parents and their children – mother and father have to be able to take over each other's roles in emergencies, which tends to reduce differences between the sexes. Whereas in a more extended family structure, which has closer ties with a wider network of kin, there is always a relative of the *same* sex available to take over when someone is unable to perform their role. The Taiwan family being of the latter type, Huang thinks it should be expected to foster sex-role differentiation.

Another, very tentative piece of evidence suggesting that there is a relationship between social position, perceptions of sex roles, and personality, comes from a study by Turner and Turner (1974). Black and white college students, of both sexes, were asked to rate 'Most men' and 'Most women' on a 15-item scale. In evaluating women, white men differed from black men, white women, or black women. They rated women low in qualities concerned with 'effectiveness' or 'efficiency'. This could be because 'effective' or 'instrumental' behaviour on the part of women in the American culture is both more common and more accepted among black people than among white people since, historically black women have usually had to work.

How 'true' are the stereotypes?

When people say that they think that women, in general, are different from men, in general, what do they really mean by this and what does it tell us? Are they simply reporting that they have observed as a matter of practical fact, that the women they have encountered tend to be such and such? Or do they mean more than this? That it is because of their biology, or genetics, or whatever, that women must always, and in any society be so? Or yet again, do they mean that *ideally* all women should be so?

Tavris (1973) points out that 'sex-role questionnaires' such as the ones used in the studies described above, do not tell us the answer to these sorts of questions. To take them as evidence of 'stereotyping' may be unfair. She therefore devised a questionnaire which appeared in *Psychology Today* (1971). It asked first, whether men and women differed in certain personality traits and second, what the differences, if any, were due to.

From the large number of replies she selected a subsample of 849 men and 593 women for study. The respondents were given a list of eight characteristics, four of which are often seen as traditionally masculine (aggressiveness, independence, objectivity, mathematical reasoning) and four which are seen as traditionally feminine (nurturance, empathy, monogamy, emotionality). They were asked whether each characteristic was more likely to be found in men, in women, or both, and, if it did occur in one sex more than the other, was this for biological or cultural reasons? She points out that this group is not representative of the general American public. *Psychology Today* readers are younger and better educated, have higher incomes, and more liberal political and religious attitudes than the average American. Also, those who replied were people who were particularly interested in Women's Liberation whether for or against. We cannot really compare their answers directly with the studies described above. However, they do illustrate the very different meanings that people may give to the 'same' observations.

As many as 80 per cent of the respondents thought that men and women differ on most of the eight traits, but not necessarily for the same reasons. About 5 per cent of men and women thought that there were sex differences on *all* eight traits, and that they were *all* due to biology. About 7 per cent thought that they were *all* due to cultural influences. Roughly one quarter saw the differences as primarily cultural. It is interesting that the people who thought that there were differences on all traits, but that these were due to culture not biology, were the most likely to be supporters of the Women's Liberation movement.

A large majority of both sexes, thought that aggressiveness was a male trait, but for cultural reasons. However, 19·6 per cent of men, and 13 per cent of women, did think that men were biologically disposed to be more aggressive. Nurturance was thought to be more characteristic of women for cultural reasons, by 35·9 per cent of men, and by 46·5 per cent of women, and for biological reasons by 31·8 per cent of men, and 26·3 per cent of women.

These are the answers of a relatively 'liberal' group of people (though even among these plenty of traditional views seem to be going strong). They demonstrate the difficulty of determining the 'truth' of popular beliefs, or stereotypes. People subscribe to them but for different reasons.

We cannot, of course, tell whether some common beliefs about women's personalities reflect biological 'truths', since nearly every society sets out to ensure that men and women grow up differently from each other. But from the evidence so far we can say that, first, both women and men do not see themselves as entirely resembling the 'stereotype' for their sex and second, that the stereotypes are influenced by the cultural roles that women and men have.

The influence of stereotypes

However, the problem with stereotypes, is that they are *not* simply cool, objective descriptions or observations of the present state of affairs. Despite Tavris's findings (1973) that some of her respondents attributed sex differences to cultural influences, there is evidence to suggest the stereotypical beliefs work to maintain existing sex roles. What pretends to be simply description ends up as prescription – 'is' becomes 'ought'. And the belief that women 'ought' to be a certain way influences them to behave appropriately (thus confirming the stereotype) and to see themselves that way.

One study which suggests that the supposedly 'typical' female characteristics are commonly seen not merely as typical but also as desirable for women, is that of Elman, Press, and Rosenkrantz (1970). When they asked a group of men and women to indicate what the ideal man and woman are like, they found that the ideal woman was seen as 'significantly less aggressive, less independent, less dominant, less active, more emotional, having greater difficulty in making decisions, etc., than the ideal man . . .' (Elman, Press, and Rosenkrantz 1970:69). The ideal man was seen as 'significantly less religious, less neat, less gentle, less aware of the feelings of others, less expressive, etc., than the ideal woman' (Elman, Press, and Rosenkrantz 1970:69).

These are the traits that also made up the stereotype. It will be remembered that Rosenkrantz found that the characteristics which were supposed to be typical of men, and some of those which were supposed to be typical of women, were also seen as socially desirable for people in general. It seems, however, that there are some socially desirable qualities that women are not supposed to possess.

Several studies show that women may see a discrepancy between the way they are, the way they want to be, and the way men want them to be. For example, Steinmann, Levi, and Fox (1964) found that women college students thought that men would ideally like women to be significantly more passive and accepting of a subordinate role in personal development and in the family, than they themselves thought they were or should be. The women may have been wrong of course – but the study by Elman, Press, and Rosenkrantz (1970) suggests that they were not all that wrong.

The finding of Rosenkrantz, that women's and men's self-concepts differ in the same direction as the stereotypes, though not to the same degree, could be interpreted to mean that both sexes are to some extent being influenced in their self-perceptions by stereotypical beliefs. Some of the conflicts for women that arise from the difference between self-concept and stereotypical beliefs, and some of the ways in which they are influenced to conform, will be discussed below, in Chapters 5 and 6.

Another curious point about stereotypes is that they seem to influence what people 'see'. Goldberg (1968) describes a study of 140 college girls.

They were told to read articles in the booklet before them, and in which 'you will find excerpts from six articles, written by six different authors in six different professional fields. At the end of each article you will find several questions ... you are not presumed to be sophisticated or knowledgeable in all the fields. We are interested in the ability of college students to make critical evaluations ...' But unbeknownst to the students, half of them had article A written by a man, and the other half were presented with the same article A but as if written by a woman and so on for all six articles.

To his expressed surprise, the articles by female authors were generally rated poorer in all respects. There were nine questions to be answered by each student for each of the six articles, thus making a total of fifty-four points at which male and female authors could be compared. Of these fifty-four comparisons, three were tied, seven favoured the female authors, and forty-four favoured the male authors. Goldberg had hypothesized that as the field of work became more generally 'female' so any favouring of males would decrease. But he found that 'Women seem to think that men are better at *everything* – including elementary-school teaching and dietetics!' The same result was found when the judgments were of contemporary paintings (Pheterson, Kiesler, and Goldberg 1971).

However, Mischel (1974) came up with a rather different finding, in a closely similar study of male and female American college students and high-school students. She did indeed find that they showed sex bias in judging journal articles – but they tended to think more highly of authors whose sex was associated with the particular field. Thus, for example, an article on dietetics was rated higher when the students thought that it had been written by a woman, and an article on city-planning was rated higher when they thought that it had been written by a man! It looks rather as if women and men who cross sex lines in their activities, run the risk of being seen as less capable, regardless of what they actually do. If this were so, it would be one more reason why stereotypical beliefs are hard to fight – people distort the evidence before their eyes.

Are women seen as 'inferior'?

So far, the evidence suggests that women in general are seen as having different personal characteristics from men. The evidence also suggests that many people think that, ideally, they should have some qualities and not others, and when they do not have them they are evaluated negatively and pressurized to conform.

Does this mean that women are being seen as 'inferior' to men? This is actually a rather complicated question. Certain supposedly 'female' qualities are clearly highly valued, for example, being aware of others' feelings, 'emotional expressiveness', and so on. The catch is that women are also thought not to possess, and at the same time not supposed to possess, other highly valued qualities such as competence, dominance, independence, aggression. What is still not clear, however, is whether women are valued less, overall.

In our view, the stereotype is peculiarly disabling. Women are valued for a rather narrow set of personal qualities. Indeed, being valued for these particular qualities (some of which are desirable in themselves, and for men as well as women) may itself be a problem. For women are supposed to restrict themselves to pursuing the 'feminine' virtues. Someone once said that sitting on a pedestal leaves you very little room for manoeuvre. There are qualities that can be regarded as vital for any individual who has found personal independence and responsibility. But these are the very qualities that women must avoid lest they be thought 'masculine'.

Many people, among them literary authors and psychological researchers, have thought that the qualities which our society considers 'masculine' and 'feminine' are not logically opposites – people can show both sorts of qualities at different times. Most research, and most so-called measures of 'masculinity–femininity', make the assumption that being 'more' masculine in personality entails being 'less' feminine. So, getting a high masculine score automatically gives a person a low feminine score. But a review of the literature led Constantinople (1973) to conclude that femininity is not the opposite of masculinity. Bem (1974) devised a measure which showed the same thing. The dimensions of masculinity and femininity were empirically independent – individuals could, and did, score high on the supposedly 'masculine' virtues, and on the 'feminine' virtues as well. Bem called this 'psychological androgyny'. She suggests that it may be adaptive and desirable for a person to show a balance of 'masculine' and 'feminine' qualities, depending on the situation. It need not mean the person is 'maladjusted' as people have sometimes thought.

Limitations of the evidence

There is an important qualification to be made about all this. We know most about the attitudes and values of American college students – a group of people who are accessible to research workers. However, though interesting in themselves, they cannot on any count be regarded as representative. We know a good deal less about other sorts of people. The beliefs, evaluations, and self-concepts of other men and women may well be very different, for instance, among less educated people, or among older people who have had to live by the consequences of their beliefs. Take, for example, the question of whether women are seen as 'inferior'. Data from American college students do not show that women are thought vastly inferior across the board. But a look at history, literature, law, and everyday life clearly shows that women have been and are, treated as inferior in many ways.

This is not a plea for simply extending the sex-role stereotype research to ever larger and supposedly more representative samples of people. For the problem with the research so far, is that it tells us almost nothing about why a particular social group sees the personalities of women, and men, in its own particular way.

Massive research on personality stereotypes alone will not help here. In the end, comparing American college students with the old, the less educated, the black Americans, or the Chinese, shows only that they agree in some ways and differ in others. We need to understand better the relationship between the *roles* expected of women, in a given society and economy, and the way they are seen as *people* by themselves and others. Smaller and more intensive investigations of people's experiences, in the world that they know, might throw more light, for instance, on why some black college students see women as more 'effective' than some white students do; or, on the reasons which lead some people to explain women's nurturance as due to culture, and others to put it down to biology.

Speculating, we suggest that the view of the 'feminine' personality held by college students, fits in well with their view of 'feminine' roles. Women are discouraged from showing personal qualities – too much independence, or competence – which might lead them to question their allotted place. They are expected to be wives, mothers, and houseworkers, only, or first and foremost. And they are supposed to fit in anything else as an 'extra', at their own cost, if at all. So it is convenient when women see themselves this way.

For women do accept stereotypes about women. Perhaps, when the social world is organized to make these stereotypes seem reasonable, even desirable, it would be surprising if they did not. Social roles, personality stereotypes, and self-images interlock. Each becomes evidence and justification for the rest.

Nonetheless, many women do seem to view their image with reservation; many experience conflict; some set out to change the image – as we shall see (Chapter 7).

FOUR

The development of sex-role perceptions

How did I come to view myself as I do? How did I develop my self-concept? Who knows? The simple answer is that no one knows. The question we ask of the research literature is whether there is any evidence to suggest how and why it is that women come to adopt roles in life that society has decreed for them. Also, whether there is anything to indicate why women come to share with other women the stereotyped view of their sex and, to some extent, of themselves. As we look at the various studies, we will keep in mind the knowledge that by the time an individual is adult he and she have clearly defined views on what is the right and wrong behaviour for each sex and the type of personality structure that goes with each.

Although we are not going to look at theories concerning self-concepts, that does not mean we are without a theory concerning the psychological development of children. Our construct theory bias (Kelly 1955) leads us to look at what people make of their world from their own point of view, rather than how we interpret each other's behaviour. When a child is not learning to read as fast as we would like, a construct theorist would not call him lazy or unintelligent, but might ask him his views on reading. Is it something he wants to do? Does he like the teacher? What does he think may happen when he is able to read?

Construct theory and self-concept development

From its earliest days, the child can be thought of as looking at its world and seeing or interpreting the consequences of its behaviour. Dropping the rattle out of the pram sometimes makes mummy laugh and sometimes produces a slap. In time it seems to the child that a laugh comes when other people are there and a slap when child and mummy are alone. There is no reason to suppose that children do not construe the similarities and differences between events in their environments before they have developed language. Far from it. Constructs are simply the discriminations we make between events in our environment and through which we look at subsequent events and so predict their outcome.

As yet only a start has been made in unravelling the complexities of ideas of self-development. But few would doubt that it has a great deal to do with how other people treat us and, more importantly, how we interpret that treatment. Salmon (1970) attempted an outline of how the child develops its interpersonal construing in construct theory terms.

First of all the baby views and organizes his world through the eyes of his mother (or permanent adult figure). However imperfectly the baby may do this, his first ideas about himself will be the ideas his mother has of him. Then others come into his life and they will be construed by him as more or less like *mother*. The baby makes no attempt to understand mother or mother-like people, he is only concerned about their behaviour in relation to himself. But as the child develops, there comes a time when there are attempts to 'see' mother's view of things and the views of others. This role construing develops as we attempt to understand the construction processes of another. The better we are able to do this, the better able we will be to predict that other's behaviour. We have entered the world of interpersonal relations. We can speculate that the more the father has to do with the early childrearing, the more varied will be the child's psychological experiences, which will greatly influence his later interpersonal relations.

As the child gets older he can see whether the constructs he has learned at his mother's knee are still valid, or whether they need altering in the light of present outcomes. But by a very early age, little girls and little boys have probably come to construe that certain behaviours are permitted for them and others only for the opposite sex. The pink bootees peeping out of the bottom of the cot will come to mean that others will respond to your babbling over a doll with smiles and other signs of approval, whereas having a go at the Meccano set may, at best, give rise to silent looks. When the whole of society colludes in this conspiracy, there is little hope for the child but to learn the lesson well. The parent who tries to break out of the stereotyped behaviour will have a child who is going to suffer because everyone else she meets will be playing by the rules. The parents who tell their child the truth about Father Christmas will be doing no harm within their own home, but what of the reactions of other parents and other children when this child insists on going around telling everyone the 'truth'?

Sex typing

We have no real evidence (only speculations) on the impact of pink and blue bootees, naming, and general cultural expectations. But it is not unreasonable to guess that parents generally play a very important part. Nevertheless, there have been innumerable studies seeking to demonstrate early differences between boys and girls at play and at work. The results add up to a resounding 'lack of differences' between boys and girls, in a psychological sense. The only relatively consistent findings concern the observations that aggressiveness appears more common in boys and verbal ability greater in girls, as well as one or two other differences of that sort (see Maccoby and Jacklin 1975 for a review of the literature).

But we are concerned here with how girls come to perceive

themselves as they do, and not specifically concerned with observed behaviour. It was Kohlberg's view (1966) that children do not have an idea about the concept of sex differences until they are of an age when it is possible to think of objects as having permanence. Piaget's concept of conservation is one of a child able to say that a quantity of water remains the same when it is transferred from a squat, wide container into a tall, narrow container. Thus the concept of sex constancy would be said to exist when the child says a doll is a girl irrespective of the changing of her clothes, hair cut, or face paint. As evidence for this view, Kohlberg cites the findings that four- to six-year-olds do think that people change their sex if outward appearance changes.

However, Thompson and Bentler (1973) found the contrary. They asked 144 children between the ages of four and six, plus ninety adults: (1) could they be a mother or a father if they wanted to be?; (2) were they going to be a mother or a father?; (3) which parent did they prefer? The children were then shown a series of twenty-four pictures, twelve representing 'masculine' items, and twelve 'feminine' items. Nineteen children and fourteen adults said they could be the parent of the opposite sex! This is a marvellous example of the ambiguity of standard questions, for they can mean different things to different people.

Thompson and Bentler reasonably suggest that the adults may have been thinking in terms of playing the role of mother or father, rather than of changing sex. It is to be hoped that this is the case, otherwise one would be justified in saying that the authors had found a somewhat biased sample of people. There is a slight relationship with age here, in that 29 per cent of the four-year-old girls thought they could change, 8 per cent of five-year-olds, increasing to 17 per cent for six-year-olds. The boys and men maintained a steady 8 per cent no matter what the age. The data allow one to do nothing but speculate. Perhaps these young girls, who develop verbally (and hence perhaps cognitively) more quickly, were using the 'role' idea more than the boys? They were saying they could change, not because the male role is more attractive (as suggested by Thompson and Bentler, but not wholly supported by their data) but because they were coming to see the role margins blurred.

Thompson and Bentler are surely right to stress that the child's belief in the possibility of sex-role swapping should not be used as the 'exclusive' means of identifying childhood transsexuals. But we lose sympathy with them in their conclusion that it could, at best, be just one indicator to 'be assessed in the context of other symptoms'. For, far from being a symptom, could it not be that these children – more girls than boys – just have a better developed idea of the nature of social roles – that they are just more aware of the social context in which they live? If this is the case, they were simply acting like the 13 per cent of adults who felt the same way.

The study of play and the sorts of sex-related toys that children use has been a profitable area of study, but research has usually been carried out to lend support for one type of theory concerning development of sex-typed behaviours as against another. It is worthwhile having a look at a few of these pieces of research in the hope that one will be offered a glimpse of what the children think they are doing when they choose to play with dolls instead of guns.

Wolf (1973) for instance, favours the social learning theory approach (see Mischel 1970). Basically, this says that a child will play with a gun not because he sees himself as a boy and 'knows' that boys play with guns, but rather that the behaviour is the result of his past learning history – he will have been rewarded relatively consistently in the past for sex-appropriate behaviour. As support for this view, Wolf had sixty seven- to eleven-year-old boys and girls watch a boy or a girl (depending on whether the child being studied was a boy or a girl) play with a toy that adults would consider inappropriate (ovens for boys and trucks for girls). When each child had watched the model play with the sex-inappropriate toy, she was observed for five minutes to see how long it was before she touched the toy, and the total time she spent playing with it. To cut a rather complicated experiment short, there were no sex differences on the latency or duration-of-play measures, but both boys and girls played with the sex-inappropriate toy longer when they observed a model doing so who was of the same sex as themselves.

Wolf then carried out another similar experiment (1974).

Only this time the 140 five- to nine-year-olds watched a boy playing with a doll and a girl with a fire-engine on videotape. The models were either praised, criticized, or not reinforced while playing with the toy. Measures were the same as in the previous experiment, that is, latency and duration-of-play. The children were asked if they liked the model and also asked to demonstrate as many of the 'unusual' acts performed by the model as possible. Both the boys and the girls played with the sex-inappropriate toy longer, having watched the same-sexed model, as opposed to the opposite-sexed, do the same, but girls touched the inappropriate toy longer and more readily than did the boys. The girls liked the model more than did the boys and they preferred the girl model to the boy model.

In an earlier study, Hartup, Moore, and Sager (1963) reported that little girls do not avoid masculine toys to the extent that boys avoid feminine ones. But they point out that many theories focus on the avoidance of sex-inappropriate behaviour rather than approach to the sex-appropriate. Their experiment was designed to see the extent to which children avoided opposite-sex behaviour as a function of age and the presence or absence of an adult. They found that boys were more reluctant to approach feminine toys as they increased in age from three to eight, and were even more reluctant when an adult was present. Not so for girls. But they did find that the frequency with which they played with inappropriate toys decreased with age in both boys and girls and this was independent of whether an adult was present or not.

All the adults used were women. Hartup, Moore, and Sager comment: '... is a permissive female examiner an irrelevant stimulus in this culture for sex-role conformity in young girls?' Girls do seem to get the message in the end, but there is much less pressure for girls to conform when surrounded by 'permissive' females right up to secondary school. This applies equally with other behaviours. A fair amount of tomboyish behaviour is tolerated in girls but 'sissy' boys get a hard time of it. Bem (1975) points out that the greater preference for sex-appropriate activities extends to college age – men chose masculine over feminine activities even when *paid* more for performing feminine activities – this was thought especially striking because the men chose tasks to maximize monetary reward considerably more than women.

The sum total of these and many other studies seems to be that girls are much more ready to play with boys' toys than boys are to play with dolls. It seems equally unlikely that this can come about through a process of modelling as some argue, because the differential selection of sex-related toys happens well before fathers spend an increasing amount of time with their sons. Is it not more likely that the child develops some notion of his sex identity via the great pressure of *mother*? It is she who persuades Johnnie to have a fire engine to go with his blue bootees and denies him the freedom to play with his sister's doll. She imposes her male stereotype on to her son right from the year dot. He comes to construe dolls as bad for him and good for Jane. For Jane, the world of toyland is different. She is given more scope. This, of course, provides no real answer since we now have to explain why mothers act this way – thus perpetuating the stereotypic rules.

Children's views of parents

There are a number of studies that describe how parents perceive children, but only a few on what children think of parents. More than twenty years ago, Ausubel and his colleagues (1954) expressed this point of view quite clearly.

'The use of children's perceptions of parent attitudes and behaviour as the independent variable, instead of measures based upon actual behaviour (or attitudes) of parents as reported by them ... or as rated by observers ... is predicated upon two assumptions. First, although parent behaviour is an objective event in the real world, it affects the child's ego development only to the extent *and in the form in which he perceives it*. Hence, perceived parent behaviour is in reality a more direct, relevant and proximate determinant of personality development than the actual stimulus content to which it refers.' (Ausubel *et al*. 1954:173, our italics)

Ausubel is thus saying that a good reason for asking the children what they think of the parents is that this is likely to be a more valid measure. Parents rating certain characteristics of their children or answering questions will be likely to be influenced by the desire to 'look good'. But the children's reports on their attitudes to parents cannot easily be validated either, since the only criteria available are the parents' own views. So we must take the reports at face value.

What Ausubel did was to take forty children from lower middle-class and working-class homes and ask them to complete stories and to fill up rating scales, concerning what they thought their parents attitudes to them were. It was then possible to derive measures of perceived acceptance and rejection, of how much the children valued themselves, and of how much they thought others valued them. The average age of the boys and girls was just over ten years. For our purposes here, the important finding was that the girls saw themselves as significantly more accepted, and valued themselves more than did the boys. Acceptance and belief in their own value correlated 0·91, showing these two things were very similar in the children's eyes.

However, eleven years before Ausubel, Meltzer (1943) had asked himself whether boys and girls differed in their fundamental attitudes and feelings for their parents. He interviewed seventy-six boys and seventy-four girls individually, asking them to shout out the first ten words that came into their heads in response to a word from the interviewer. He felt that 'At best the method yields a dynamic sampling of all interacting processes of child and parent as perceived by the child. At worst it yields a fair picture of fixed attitudes and stereotypes acquired by the child' (Meltzer 1943:314). These children ranged in age from nine to fifteen years.

One difference between mothers and fathers when all responses had been classified under thirteen headings, was that both boys and girls thought that mothers 'do things for you', whereas fathers do less than mothers, particularly in the eyes of girls. Girls, however, saw fathers as being there 'to take care of you'. Father rather than mother is a person who 'takes me places', 'gives me things', and 'plays with me' in the eyes of both boys and girls. Mother is more often described in terms of personality characteristics, and father in terms of physical ones. What Meltzer classifies as emotional responses, are more common in girls than in boys, and applied by both more commonly to mother than to father. Thus, mother works *for* you, has a personality, and is responded to emotionally, whereas father does things *with* you, and has a physique.

Meltzer then analysed the types of feeling the children had for their parents. He found that girls had more pleasant feelings towards both parents than did the boys. Both boys and girls expressed more pleasant feelings towards mother than towards father. In terms of type of feelings ranging from hostility to admiration and adoration, both boys and girls reacted more favourably to mother than to father. In a more detailed analysis of each category of response, girls had more hostility feelings to mother than to father and boys more to father than to mother. Thus it seems that both boys and girls are more favourably disposed to mother than to father, but whenever hostility exists, it is directed towards the same-sexed parent.

Mothers were preferred to fathers by both boys and girls at all ages in Thompson and Bentler's study (1973). But the boys' preference for fathers was greater than the girls', although girls increased their preference for father as they aged from four to six years. Around 30 per cent of the 144 children said they had no preference. But taking an overview of all studies, it does seem that mother scores more points than father in the eyes of young children.

Jourard and Remy (1955) linked how adolescents and adults evaluate their parents with their feelings of security.

> 'Personal security may be defined as the belief that one is adequate to handle life problems, and that one is well liked both by oneself and by significant others. According to this definition, we would expect that a person who believes that his parents evaluate him positively, and who evaluates himself positively, would be secure.'
>
> (Jourard and Renny 1955:364)

So they set out to see how fifty-one female and forty-eight male college students aged between eighteen to twenty-eight viewed their bodies and themselves. This was then related to how they thought their parents had evaluated them and their bodies. There were indeed significant relationships between perceived

63

views of self and body and perceived mothers' and fathers' views, and these in turn correlated significantly with feelings of security. They comment that the relationship was a much firmer one for the women than for the men.

Children's views of teachers

In general it seems that mothers are more important than fathers in the eyes of young children, and that girls see themselves as being accepted more by their parents than do boys and evaluate themselves more highly, which in turn may be linked to feelings of security.

This preferred evaluation of girls over boys can be seen in the school as well as in the home. Davidson and Lang (1960) studied how children perceived their teacher's perceptions of them. They tested three specific hypotheses: (1) that there would be a positive correlation between children's perception of their teacher's feelings towards them and how the children saw themselves; (2) that there would be a positive relationship between a favourable perception of the teacher's feelings and good academic achievement; and (3) that there would be a positive relationship between a favourable perception of the teacher's feelings and desirable classroom behaviour.

The children were given a list of thirty-five words, some favourable and others unfavourable, such as 'fair', 'a nuisance', 'careless'. They were asked to decide how the teacher felt about them in respect to each word and then to rate it on a 3-point scale (most of the time, half the time, and seldom or almost never). Eighty-nine boys and 114 girls did this in fourth, fifth, and sixth grades in a New York public school. The socio-economic status of the children ranged from sixty-three coming from professional families to eighty-three from semi-skilled or unskilled families. The children worked on the list twice, once filling it out 'as my teacher thinks I am', and the second time 'as I think I am'. The teachers rated the children on academic achievement on a 4-point scale ranging from 'doing very well' to 'doing very poorly'. Teachers also rated the children on ten behavioural and personality characteristics, scored according to whether they were judged desirable or undesirable.

The results were in accord with the hypotheses. There was a correlation of 0·82 between the children's perception of themselves and of their perception of the teacher's view of them. That is, the more favourable the child's own self-concept, the better he thought the teacher's view of him. This is very much in accord with the findings of Ausubel *et al.* (1954) and of Jourard and Remy (1955). Here is support for the view that one of the roles of a teacher is as a parent substitute. Also, that one's self-concept is related to what 'significant others' think of one.

Perhaps of even greater interest is the finding that the more favourably perceived by the teacher the child *thinks* he is, the better assessed are his academic achievement and classroom behaviour. As girls perceived their teacher's feelings towards them to be more favourable than did the boys, so their behaviour ratings were also more favourable. They were rated more highly too on achievement, although not significantly so. Thus, girls live in a climate of approval for a much longer period during childhood than do boys. They perceive more acceptance from mothers than from fathers, and also expect more favourable reactions from teachers than boys do, since most primary school teachers are women. Since they have the approval of the 'authority figure' they do not have to, or do not feel the same compulsion to, compete as do boys in the same class as these 'favoured' girls.

The question of the perceived desirability of competition and its possible relationship to academic achievement will be dealt with in detail separately in Chapter 5. Now we want to pursue the idea of the interaction between pupil and teacher and the possible effects of this on the behaviour of boys and girls.

Nash (1973) in his book *Classrooms Observed* reports on his study of one class of children as they pass from an English primary to a secondary school. One of his hypotheses was that 'behaviour of children in classes where they are perceived unfavourably by the teacher will be different from their behaviour in classes where they are perceived favourably' (Nash 1973:65).

To obtain a measure of attitudes to the children, Nash gave three of the teachers a form of repertory grid in which the constructs were elicited and the children were the elements. The repertory grid has undergone many changes since it was first described by Kelly (1955) as a means of quantifying the relationships between the units of his theory – the construct. Since it is the only method other than the Rosenkrantz Questionnaire, that has been used in several studies to be discussed in this book, it is worth a brief explanation.

All forms of grid require the person to sort certain ideas or objects in terms of other ideas or *constructs*. Thus, if you are interested in people's attitudes to films, you can have a set of films that you think cover a fair range, and ask the person to rank or rate these films in terms of certain constructs given to you by the individual, or else supplied by you. Thus, the films can be ranked in terms of the amount of *violence*, *sex*, *artistry*, or *technical merit*, or anything else you like. The degree to which these rankings are similar or dissimilar can be stated in mathematical terms. The resulting correlations give an indication of how the constructs relate to each other for each individual. The argument goes that if the ranking of the films on *violence* is almost identical to the ranking of the films on *sex*, then this statistical relationship corresponds to a psychological relationship. This person thinks that *sex* and *violence* go hand in hand. (All sorts of measures have been derived from such grids. Further descriptions of the procedures and measures can be found in Fransella and Bannister 1977.)

Nash obtained a measure of 'favourability' from his grid with teachers. As a result of the analysis he came to the conclusion that, 'sometimes teachers perceived girls so much more favourably than boys that a boy might have construct rank 10, and yet, since the first nine ranks are given to girls, be the most favourably perceived boy in class' (Nash 1973:66).

In another part of the study, Nash looked at fifteen children in a remedial reading class. He found that they were not only bottom of the class but were also perceived very unfavourably. They were construed as dull, less capable, troublesome, badly behaved, and also passive, stolid, immature, and less interesting. So not only were these disadvantaged children seen as having low ability, they were also negatively perceived in other respects.

To look more deeply at this, Nash took a group of children matched with the remedial group for intelligence, but who were not in a remedial class. The results are set out in *Table 5*.

Table 5 Class position and favourability ratings for children in a remedial and non-remedial class.

N	mean IQ	social class	primary class position	fav: rank
Remedial class children				
boys 8	81	7	30	28
girls 7	79	7	31	28
Non-remedial class children				
boys 8	79	7	29	20
girls 7	81	7	23	11

(Source: Nash 1973:85–86)

Nash argues that the girls being ranked twenty-third in class position compared with the boys' rank of twenty-ninth, cannot account for the marked discrepancy in favourability ranking. It does look as if the girls of low IQ who were favourably perceived by teacher, did not go into remedial class. This becomes important in relation to Nash's finding that by the age of eight, academic self-perception correlates significantly with teacher's perception.

One further finding of interest here is that the children's perception of themselves correlated 0·72 with the other children's perceptions of them. For example, if six children see John as being cleverer than they are, there will be a reasonable chance that John will see himself as being cleverer than they are.

In a much earlier study, Brandt (1958) looked to see whether there was any difference in the accuracy with which boys and girls assessed their abilities and social reputations. He took 139 children from sixth and eleventh grades and asked each to state whether he or she expected to do better than each class-mate. Each then carried out academic and physical tasks against which the accuracy of their self-estimate was assessed. He found that the boys were significantly more accurate in their estimates of achievement than the girls when in the sixth grade.

(Unfortunately it proved not to be possible to compare the eleventh grade children.) Also 50 per cent of the boys, as compared with 25 per cent of the girls overestimated themselves. Brandt makes the point that 'self-estimates should not be separated from estimates of other people; rather, they are but two aspects of the same perceptual process. The self-concept develops in a social matrix as the individual sees himself in relation to other people and as he perceives other people viewing him' (Brandt 1958:73).

Thus, if our self-concepts develop, in part at least, in relation to how we think authority figures and our contemporaries perceive us, then girls in primary schools with mixed classes are off to a good start.

It is not only in England that girls are more likely to be teachers' pets. In an American study of 1,748 ten- and eleven-year-old children, Coopersmith (1967) found that teachers' ratings of girls were much more favourable than their ratings for boys. Yet, interestingly, he did not find that these differences had produced any measurable difference between boys and girls in self-esteem (see Chapter 6).

This lack of difference between the boys and girls in how they value themselves could be due to changes in culture and changes in upbringing since the 1950s. But there is evidence that girls do see themselves nearer their ideal than do boys. For example, Perkins (1958) looked at the relationship between the perception of self and of ideal self in 251 children in fourth grade classes and then tested them again when they were in the sixth grade. He defined self as 'those perceptions, beliefs, feelings, attitudes and values which the individual views as describing himself. The ideal self was defined in terms of those qualities which describe the person he would like to be' (Perkins 1958:221).

Perkins had the children sort fifty self-referent statements chosen from a large number collected from fourth and sixth grade children. The sorts for self and ideal self were correlated to give a measure of 'congruency'. The two findings that are relevant here are that the girls were significantly more 'congruent' than the boys and that the congruency increased from fourth to sixth grade. The measure was independent of intelligence but was significantly related to whether female teachers had had the opportunity to take a course in child study. The better the teacher the higher the girls valued themselves. But the question remains—how was this achieved? As yet there is no answer.

One of the few longitudinal studies looking at how children's views and self-satisfactions change as they grow up is that carried out in London. Moore and Clautour (1977) report on the replies of the same sixty-eight boys and forty-eight girls when at ages seven, twelve, and fifteen. When aged seven, these London-born children gave a resounding positive reply when asked whether they liked their present age. But only a small majority of them liked being twelve, and at fifteen the number satisfied were in a minority. In fact, at both twelve and fifteen years old, 30 per cent gave an unreserved negative reply.

At all ages between 80 per cent and 90 per cent preferred to be their own sex. However, 13 per cent of the girls at both twelve and fifteen wanted to be boys, whereas the figure for boys wanting to be girls at those ages was 1 per cent and 3 per cent.

Of particular interest were the replies to the question concerning preference for a man's or a woman's life. At seven years of age there is no problem; boys want a man's life and girls want a woman's. At twelve, about half of both boys and girls are undecided, 21 per cent of boys want a woman's life, and 19 per cent of girls want a man's life. But by the age of fifteen, only 12 per cent of boys want a woman's life and an impressive 40 per cent of girls want a man's life. Moore and Clautour's account of the reasons given for these preferences makes interesting reading:

' "An easier life" was mentioned (more often than an interesting life) by each sex as an advantage of the opposite one: a man's life is easier because it is freer, said several girls – "if he wants to, he goes out, but the woman has to stay in and look after the children" and boys at 15 tended to agree: but women have fewer responsibilities, "they are taken everywhere and paid for", and some girls liked this. Some boys and a handful of girls at 15 did speak of the more interesting careers open to men, and of financial independence; but dislike of the work of the opposite sex figured among both boys and girls as a reason for preferring one's own; and vice versa. Yet only three girls at 12, and again at 15, explicitly preferred the homemaking role. Again, we note that work of any kind is not a welcome thought.'

(Moore and Clautour 1977)

Adolescence

Lifshitz (1976) studied college students – this time Israeli undergraduate women studying psychology. She used a questionnaire consisting of thirty-seven items (eighteen feminine and nineteen masculine) from the Rosenkrantz Questionnaire which had been adapted for Israelis. The items were listed in columns and the students had to mark those three characteristics that best represented their mother, their father, those they would like their mother to have, those they would most like their father to have, and lastly those they themselves would most like to have. They were required to place a plus against those characteristics that were thought desirable and a minus for those thought undesirable.

All girls saw their mothers and ideal mothers as having significantly more feminine than masculine characteristics, except for only-child girls whose ideal mothers did not have significantly more feminine characteristics. But fathers for all girls, regardless of birth order, were not seen as having more significantly masculine than feminine characteristics. Lifshitz's findings also supported those of Rosenkrantz in showing that stereotyped masculine characteristics are generally considered more socially desirable than are feminine ones.

Lifshitz thinks that sex-role identification is a process of perceptual differentiation and integration of personality characteristics of which the person is aware and which develops within the nuclear family. She looked at the literature and concluded that women and girls have a less clearly defined view of females than do boys. But others (for example, Biller 1973; Goldberg and Lewis 1969) have found a clearly dichotomized bisexual picture. It must be remembered that all the studies Lifshitz cites are on Israeli women and children. It has been found that college-graduate women tend to identify with their fathers rather than with their mothers (e.g. Patrick 1972).

She hypothesizes that girls strive to integrate both the feminine and masculine roles in their way of life. She also argues
that first-born girls or only-child girls will place a higher value
on intellectual and social responsibility – a characteristic more
commonly attributed to males. Thus first-born girls will try to
emulate perceived characteristics in *both* parents rather than
those perceived in just one. Spence, Helmreich, and Stapp
(1975) support this view when disagreeing with Bem's conception of androgyny (1974) as being one of balance, and see it
rather as meaning the possession of a high degree of both
masculine and feminine characteristics.

In a previous study (1974), Lifshitz used repertory grid
technique to investigate the attitudes of some social work
students. Although not detailed in the 1974 paper, in the 1976
one she states that:

'a group of social work students (mean age 22·7) described
their fathers as the ideal figure, and it seemed that according
to his attributes they selected their mate. When the students
were compared with their supervisors (mean age 39·9) it was
found that as the father had become more and more removed
in time from the girls' life, his desirable attributes were
further transferred to the husband, as well as being internalized by the subject herself.'   (Lifshitz 1976)

Let us take this as an idea, rather than a scientific fact of life,
and extend it. Boys develop a self-concept of themselves as boys
and are like dad in having male (desirable) attributes. Girls
develop a view of themselves as girls and as being like mum in
having female attributes (not all so desirable). But a girl has
something extra. She sees dad as having both feminine as
well as masculine attributes and also holds him up as some sort
of ideal figure. She has a foot in both camps. But somewhere
along the way she realizes that dad's world is not her world.
She is forced to emphasize her feminine attributes and play
down her masculine ones.

Our evidence has led us to see girls as seeing themselves as
developing in a climate of approval. Perhaps they learn quite
early to actively seek this approval since this is frequently

rewarded. Conformity gains approval. In time this leads girl to *want* to change themselves as they get older in order to conform to the sex-role stereotypes that are now expected from them by society at large.

It is when adolescence approaches that problems emerge. Komarovsky (1946) reported that 40 per cent of the women students interviewed, at some time tried to conceal their academic prowess: 'When a girl asks me what marks I got last semester, I answer, "Not so good – only one A." When a boy asks the same question, I say very brightly with a note of surprise, "Imagine, I got an A."'

It would be nice to think that in these enlightened mid-1970s that times had changed. But in 1961, at least, Coleman states that

'... the relation between boys and girls in a middle-class school operates to make the label "brilliant student" something for a girl to shy away from, although lesser scholastic accomplishments may be desired. This is most evident in the most upper-middle-class school, Executive Heights, where not one of the 49 girls in the top leading crowd responded that she wanted to be remembered as a brilliant student.'

(Coleman 1961:248)

It would perhaps not be such a serious finding if it simply led girls to behave 'like girls', but there are more sinister implications. But just what are these sinister implications and are they indeed real?

Shaw and McCuen (1960) showed that the rot sets in early. They located 168 children who had been tested on an IQ test while in the eighth grade and who were now in the eleventh and twelfth grades. These were then grouped into 'achievers' and 'underachievers' and their academic records looked at from the first to the eleventh grade. In Figures 1 and 2 (boys and girls respectively) one can clearly see that the pattern of change is different. Boys started underachieving in the first grade and continued in the same vein. Girls, however, did not start to seriously underachieve until the sixth grade, around puberty, and were, in fact, slightly better at school work up until then. But such a finding does not help us much in trying to identify what it is in the child's view of the world that makes a child not realize its full potential.

The work of Horner (1972) attempts to get nearer to an answer. The author focused on the apparent conflict in which the successful girl may find herself when she sees she is able to do well and yet considers it unfeminine to succeed. She asked

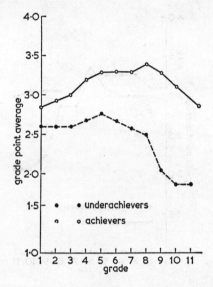

Figure 1. *Comparison of achievement at school of boys classified as 'achievers' and 'underachievers' as they moved from grade I to grade II*
(Source: Shaw and McCuen 1960:105)

adolescents to write stories about successful young men and women, describing what they are like and the sorts of things that might happen to them. She found that many of the women gave accounts of unpleasant events happening to the successful women, but very few of the men described unpleasant things happening to the successful men (see Chapter 6 for a further discussion of 'fear of success').

However, Monahan, Kuhn, and Shaver (1974) tidied up the

experimental design a little and found the now familiar stereo-type operating again. Both sexes described unpleasant futures for the successful women – boys seeing girls' futures as being even worse than did the girls themselves and both sexes being equally positive about male success. The following is one example of a boy's hostility to the successful Anne who had just

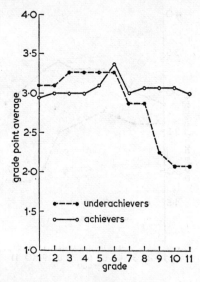

Figure 2. *Comparison of achievement at school of girls classified as 'achievers' and 'underachievers' as they moved from grade I to grade II*
(Source: Shaw and McCuen 1960:106)

heard that she had come top of her medical school: 'She is so overwhelmed she celebrates by letting all the boys lay her as she goes on studying. The future holds for Anne that she will go from whore to prostitute' (Monahan, Kuhn and Shaver 1974:64).

Wyer and Weatherley (1965) look at another aspect of aca-demic striving in women. They focus on the fact that to be dominating or striving is unfeminine, and point out that many females will adopt submissive roles on purpose so as to avoid being threatening to males (see, for example, Weiss 1961). By studying male and female students, they were able to show that successful female students felt very guilty about aggression and very seldom expressed their aggression directly.

Coleman (1961) studied how self-evaluations change over time. He says that:

'Boys and girls start very close to the same point, but then diverge, the best girl students becoming *less* likely over the four years to want to be remembered for their scholastic achievements, and the best boy students becoming *more* likely to want to be remembered in this way.'

(Coleman 1961:251)

But, in the ten schools being studied, the girls consistently acquired higher grades than did the boys. He comments:

'The double constraints upon girls – to do well but not to be brilliant – are evident in other ways as well. For many a girl, the solution to the dilemma of "good but not aggressively brilliant" is an ingenious one; she gets good grades, but she is never extremely outstanding. She is neither better than the best boy student nor poorer than the worst. Her grades are "compressed" by the double constraints of conforming to the two norms. As a result, the grades of a girl are more nearly alike from course to course than those of a boy, and the within-girl variance in grades is less than for boys. If a girl has a B average, she has more B's and fewer's C's than does a boy with a B average.' (Coleman 1961:252–53)

In one of the few cross-cultural studies, Gill and Spilka (1962) tried to relate achievement to mothers' personality. They took high school junior and senior Mexican–American children and divided them into high achievers and underachievers. They hypothesized that, among other things, achieving Mexican–Americans would come from homes in which the mothers would be more dominating, possessive, and ignore the child less.

They found, in fact, that underachieving boys and achieving girls came from homes in which the mothers were more dominating than were the mothers of achieving boys and under-

75

achieving girls. They concluded that restrictive and demanding maternal attitudes are perceived by the academically successful girl as affectionate concern for her. The daughter, therefore, may be able to identify with her mother and accept her control. It could equally well be argued that the girls perceived in these dominating mothers similar characteristics to their fathers and behaved accordingly.

Added to the apparent problems adolescent girls have about doing well educationally, they also have problems about the future. Hauser and Shapiro (1973) found that boys and girls under seventeen differed markedly in their certainty about themselves in the future. Girls are much more certain than boys as to what they will be like. But when compared with those above seventeen, the position was reversed – boys were much more certain than girls. And it is not just that boys had increased in their certainty; girls had actually reduced. Another point of interest is that the girls before seventeen had a very stable view of themselves as they thought their friends saw them. These relationships were calculated by having the adolescents rate a number of attributes obtained from listening to a group of them having a discussion. These ratings were on 9-point scales. This meant that each adolescent would first of all rate the attributes as they related to herself, then rate the same attributes again according to how she saw herself in ten years time, how her friends saw her and so forth. These girls' ratings of themselves were very similar to their ratings of how their friends saw them (>0.75). For boys the correlation was below 0.4. However, for the older than seventeen group the correlation for girls had dropped to around 0.65 and the boys risen to around 0.55.

Conclusions

We have selected studies relating as closely as possible to the topic: 'How do female children see themselves?' But there is really not very much evidence available. And what there is, is not always very illuminating or imaginative. We will end with one study of a type that might yield more relevant information in the future.

76

In 1975, Bannister tape-recorded the conversations of young children and then had the tapes transcribed. These were then read back to the children to find out whether they were able to recognize their own conversations or not. He found that girls were able to recognize themselves much more easily and at a younger age than boys. Unfortunately, there is no information yet on how they managed to do this. Such data would tell a great deal about how these children perceive themselves.

What is it that enabled the girls particularly to recognize their own styles? More research along these lines could help us answer the general questions – 'How do we come to recognize ourselves?' and 'What is it that identifies us as us?'

FIVE

College students and their careers

In Chapter 2, we saw that better educated women are generally in favour of women working outside the home. And yet highly educated women do not fulfil their potential and training in working life. In most industrialized societies fewer women than men reach university and, if they do, they are less likely to pursue their careers afterwards. Among those who do pursue careers, fewer reach 'top jobs' (see Garai and Scheinfeld 1968; Fogarty, Rapoport, and Rapoport 1971; Bernard 1966).

What are the reasons for this? External factors such as discrimination, prejudice, and practical problems are, of course, important (see O'Leary 1974; Fogarty, Rapoport, and Rapoport 1971; Hartnett 1975 for a review). But women's prejudices and their perceptions of their own personalities also play a part. For instance, a survey of American college students of both sexes (171,509 people in all) from 326 colleges, showed that about half the men and a third of the women thought 'The activities of married women are best confined to the home and family' (Wasserman 1973).

So what do college women hope for themselves in the future? What do they see as their most important roles? What would they prefer to do? What is it that makes some women choose unusual paths for themselves? Why do some become strongly committed to careers and develop interests that are uncommon for women?

Choice for future roles

Men who enter university know that they will be breadwinners even if many are not certain about precisely what they will do. For college women the picture remains less clear for much longer.

Most studies report that 'boys have a clearer concept of their future occupational roles, are more realistic in their vocational planning, and less frequently engaged in unrealistic fantasies and pipedreams about future happiness than girls' (Garai and Scheinfeld 1968). This is hardly surprising. Most women expect to become wives and mothers. And most people still assume that it is the woman and not the man, who should take a job only if it fits in with the needs of home and children and partners' job. Given all the unknown factors, it is realistic for women to find it more difficult to make long-term career plans.

There may, however, be more to the dilemma. Schoolgirls and women at college are showing more interest in a variety of careers (Empey 1958; Simpson and Simpson 1963). It seems as if, for some at least, college is a period in which they are still resolving major questions of identity – asking themselves, 'who am I?'. They are wondering just how important a career is to them. Are they to become wives and mothers? Or career women? Or all three? Can they really have a career *and* children? And what sort of marriage would make that possible?

To study such attitudes, Epstein and Bronzaft (1972) gave a questionnaire to 1,063 American college women. These were attending a tuition-free public university and most students came from lower-middle- and working-class backgrounds. They were asked what they would prefer to be fifteen years from now:

a housewife with no children

a housewife with one or more children
an unmarried career woman
a married career woman without children
a married career woman with children
or whether they were uncertain

Almost no one wanted to stay single – or childless. About half wanted to be a married career woman with children. A further third chose to be a housewife with one or more children. But almost one in five were not certain what they wanted from life.

In another study (Vogel *et al.* 1970) sixty-five women students at a Catholic women's college were asked how long they planned to be employed after they completed their education. All intended to do some work; 9 per cent intended to stop work at marriage; 2 per cent meant to stop work when their husbands had completed their education. But as many as 50 per cent intended to stop work when their first child was born and 39 per cent planned to continue working full-time or part-time after the birth of the children.

There is evidence that, for many women, the uncertainty about the future is not easily resolved. Angrist (1972) set out to see how women's views of themselves changed as they progressed through college. She interviewed eighty-seven women college students who entered a fairly select private college in 1964. They also filled in a questionnaire every autumn for the four college years. The questionnaire asked them what they planned to do in the future and what they hoped for. She found that all the women intended to have families. But they varied considerably as to what else they meant to do, and many of them changed their minds during the course of the four years. Some of the students (18 per cent) could be classified as 'consistent careerists'. They came to college with the intention of becoming career women as well as wives and they stuck to their intention of having a career throughout. One third started out with no intention of having a career and they held to this also. But as many as 22 per cent at first had no interest in a career but wanted one by the time they left college; 13 per cent started out with career plans but gave them up, and another 14 per cent vacillated in attitude to a career throughout the four years. In other words, in the course of their time at college, very nearly half of these women changed their minds at least once about what they wanted to be in later life.

Why is it that college students seem to be so much in doubt and for so long? A tentative reason for this indecision comes from a small pilot study by Schwenn (1970). She interviewed sixteen women at an 'outstanding eastern women's college' in America. Most students come to this college bent on a career. Yet most of them, at least the ones questioned, changed their major subjects and/or their future career plans at some time. Fourteen of them moved to what they saw as more traditionally feminine and therefore less ambitious aims. For example, one woman said, 'Law school is less ambitious, it doesn't take as long ... is more flexible in terms of marriage and children. It is less masculine in that it is accepted now for girls to go to law school' (Schwenn 1970:167). Others opted to become teachers, housewives and so on. Only two of the sixteen girls became more ambitious and moved into fields which are traditionally seen as more 'masculine'.

Thus it seems that some women give up their real interests, or the idea of a serious career, because it appears to them to conflict with their marriage prospects, and with motherhood. Nonetheless, there are others for whom college brings new possibilities. For the first time they realize that work could be important and satisfying.

A point to notice is that becoming interested in a career is, usually, adding, rather than substituting, a role to their repertory. It is very unusual, at any stage, for a woman to say that she does not intend being a wife, or mother. It is also socially unacceptable.

But do women who want to combine a career and a family have any clear idea of the practical, or personal, difficulties and conflicts that they will run into? Or how they will deal with them? Most probably they realize there are difficulties, but have only a very vague notion of what these are. They can hardly be helped by the new 'liberal' mythologies which seem to suggest that a really 'together' and capable woman will manage with a little effort, and without seriously altering her marriage role.

Why do college students choose the roles they do?

Planning to work is not the same as committing oneself to one's work. Many college women expect to work as a matter of necessity, at some stage in their lives, but intend to give it up when they marry or when the first child is born. Others see career commitment as an essential part of their own identity. They may work part-time, or stop work temporarily when their children are small, but they intend to take up their careers again later.

What, then, is it that makes some women deviate from the supposedly 'traditional' pattern? First of all, one can say that commitment to a career is related to the students' self-concepts and to their sex-role stereotypes for women in general. For example, Zissis (1962) found that career-oriented college women described themselves as 'competitive', 'aggressive', and 'managerial', whereas women who wanted only marriage saw themselves as more 'docile', 'self-effacing', and 'co-operative'.

Richardson (1975) was also interested in this question. She sent a questionnaire by mail to ninety-seven senior college women (a socio-economically stratified sample from an urban college). The questionnaire consisted of fifty-eight 7-point rating scales, each applicable to women in various roles.

Each student rated herself, rated her view of the 'ideal woman', and then went through the scales again, to describe her image of a 'career woman' (a career woman was defined as a woman with a major interest in a career, who may or may not have marriage and family responsibilities). Finally, she used the same scale to describe a 'homemaker' (homemaker was defined as a woman whose major interest is in home and family).

In a separate questionnaire, each student was asked how important a career was to her, if at all, and what her career plans were, if any.

Richardson found that women who saw themselves as most similar to the way they saw a 'homemaker' were significantly less likely to be career-oriented. A career was not important to them. This was as she had predicted.

However, women who saw themselves as most similar to their image of a 'career woman' were not more likely to be committed to a career. This was a surprising result. Richardson suggests a possible explanation: '... the developmental process for women who are deviating in some way from the traditional female role is a more difficult and prolonged one affected by a variety of internal and external factors ...' (Richardson 1975:126). In other words, when a woman knows that she does not fit the expected roles, she has got problems! She may be uncomfortable with the traditional pattern, but she still does not know how to be happy, or accepted, if she steps out of it. Compared with her, the more 'traditional' woman has an easier time of it. Her view of herself and her wishes is similar to society's view of her. She is taking a well-trodden path.

There is also some evidence for a relationship between a woman's choice of roles and the extent to which her self-image resembles the feminine personality stereotype. In the study of Catholic college women by Vogel et al. (1970), the women were asked about their plans for work, marriage, and children, and also answered Rosenkrantz's sex-role questionnaire (see Chapter 3 for a description). Each student rated an adult male, an adult female, and finally herself.

On the basis of their replies to the sex-role questionnaire, the students were divided into two groups. One group saw themselves as more similar to the 'feminine stereotype' – relatively low on competence-related traits, and high on warmth and expressiveness. The other group described themselves as less like the 'feminine stereotype' – high on competence-related traits, and lower on warmth and expressiveness.

Almost all the women wanted to be wives and mothers. But it turned out that women who had a more 'stereotypically feminine' image of their personalities, wanted significantly more children. Women who were intending to study for an advanced degree, tended to see themselves as more competent – but not less warm and expressive. Women who wanted to combine having a job, with having children, described themselves as

83

relatively less warm and expressive – but not more competent – than the women who wanted to be simply wives and mothers. Thus, women with more 'traditional' self-concepts keep to the more traditional roles.

Again, it seems that the way a woman sees her own personality influences the role she chooses. Or perhaps it is the other way round – she modifies her view of herself to fit the roles she expects for herself.

A college woman's work plans for herself are also related to her views on women's roles in general. Steinmann (1963) investigated this relationship, among other things, in a study of fifty-one middle-class American college women and their families. She thought that attitudes to a woman's role could be seen as a continuum. At one end of the continuum would be the belief that women should be 'other-oriented' and at the other extreme is the belief that women should be 'self-oriented'. By 'other-oriented' she means 'women who seek fulfilment through the intermediary of others' – they get their satisfactions mainly indirectly, from looking after husband and children, and taking pleasure in *their* achievements. By 'self-oriented' she means 'women who seek fulfilment in life by actualizing their own potentialities'.

She found that the college women who were aiming for jobs which usually require some commitment (such as teaching, social work, research, and other professions) were significantly more 'self-oriented' than the women who wanted secretarial work – this being work which women often mean to do only until they get married.

Choosing 'unfeminine' careers

Her image of herself, and her views on sex roles, influence a college woman's commitment to work. Do they also influence what subject she studies, and the type of work she chooses?

The interests and work preferences of educated women do suggest sex-role stereotyping. The average woman studies different subjects at school and at college from the average man and she goes into different jobs. Rossi (1965a) observed that only 7 per cent of American women graduates qualified in those subjects that have traditionally been thought 'masculine', especially the physical sciences. Over 70 per cent of American employed women are in only four fields – teaching, nursing, secretarial work, and social work (Tangri 1972).

Some of these differences are due to discrimination, open or hidden. But women also differ from men in their work values and interests. Over and over again, we find that women say they want to 'work with people', and men 'with things'. On the face of it, 'working with people' looks as if it fits in with the feminine stereotype – which is to be 'other-oriented' and warm and expressive.

What is it, then, that makes some women choose 'unfeminine' careers? Of course, choice of career depends on a great many things, and the process has been much less studied among women than men (Klemmack and Edwards 1973). Often, the studies produce conflicting results. However, there are some clues.

There is some evidence that a woman's family and social background make a difference to her work commitment, and perhaps too, to the type of work she chooses.

A popular myth sees women as 'abnormal' if they take their careers seriously, or choose 'unfeminine' fields. So-called experts have even suggested that they are psychologically disturbed. One hypothesis is that they are 'over-identified' with their fathers. The assumption here being that 'normal' women identify with their mothers, so that strong identification with father is unusual and perhaps pathological for a woman. Tangri (1972) reviews some of the evidence on this, and comes to the conclusion that it is ill-founded (see also Ch. 4 pp. 71–2).

For example, the authors of a study of women mathematicians thought they were unusually 'father-identified' (Plank and Plank 1954). Yet a study of adolescent girls who chose careers which are unusual for women did not find this (Douvan 1963; Douvan and Adelson 1966). Research on more creative women mathematicians (Helson 1961) gave evidence both for and against.

Identification is a curious and global concept. What does it mean? A daughter may see herself as like her father in some ways, and emulate and admire him – but this does not mean that she wants to be like him in every way. Nor need she necessarily see herself as 'masculine'. Most women who choose to work or have atypical careers want to combine the work with marriage and motherhood. Even if they are identifying with their fathers, they are identifying with their mothers as well. There is another way of looking at this. Identifying with her father to some extent could be a good thing. Choosing an unusual career is associated with greater ego-strength and higher self-esteem (see reviews of Helson 1972 and Hoffman 1972), and career commitment is associated with desire for self-fulfilment (Steinmann 1963). If these come from identifying with father, it seems to have positive results for the women concerned.

Almquist and Angrist (1970) had a different view. They suggest that college women who become career-committed, or choose atypical careers, have profited from additional and enriching experiences which the others have missed out on. They carried out an intensive study of 110 college women from a co-educational, private, selective, expensive college. Every autumn throughout their four years at college, the women answered an extensive questionnaire on their adult role conceptions, occupational choices, career plans, work experiences, school activities, dating, and social life. Each student was also interviewed twice during the four years.

It turned out that 'career-committed' and 'atypical career' choosers did deviate in some ways from the average female college student. The career-committed were significantly less likely to be going steady, engaged, or married by the senior year. But both they and the atypical career choosers dated just as often as the others. Also, their attitudes to their parents were no different from the average. Thus the main way in which these students 'deviate' is that they are less eager to be married in the near future. However, they did want to have a family as much as the rest. So the supposed deviants do not seem to be deviating very much in any important respect. Perhaps they felt in more conflict about their roles in life. But perhaps also, they felt less under pressure to marry at once, and were confident enough in themselves to postpone that decision.

The groups did, however, differ in their work values. The career-committed women more often valued work situations which would allow them to make use of their special abilities and free them from class supervision. Women who chose atypical careers more often valued work which would permit use of their special abilities and lead to a high income, less often preferred working with people (rather than with things) and working 'to help others', and were less willing to fall in with their parents' idea of success. In other words, their work values did not conform to the 'feminine' norm.

From the same study it also turned out that there was a good deal of support for the 'enrichment' hypothesis. Both career-committed and the 'atypical' women had often had experiences which the others had not. They had had, for instance, more part-time and summer jobs during the college years and they had had more varied jobs. They were twice as likely to say that they had been influenced in their work choice by someone actually doing that job, whereas the others tended to say they were influenced by family, peers – or no one. In addition to this, both career-committed and atypical career choosers more often had mothers who were employed, and who had had highter education themselves.

Perhaps, then, the horizons of these unusual women had been broadened by experience not available to most. Their own work experience helped, but they had also benefited from the experience of others – and especially of their mothers.

Tangri (1972) also investigated the question of what makes college women choose unusual work roles for themselves. She selected a group of senior students who had entered the university of Michigan four years previously, in 1963.

There were sixty-five who were classified as 'role innovators' (because they had chosen occupations with less than 30 per cent of women in them); sixty-six who were 'moderates' (they had chosen occupations with between 30 per cent and 50 per cent of women in them); and sixty-nine classified as 'traditional' (they had chosen occupations with more than 50 per cent of women in them). It is important to remember that the term 'role innovator' refers only to their work choice – nearly all the women in all groups wanted to marry and have children.

A questionnaire covering family background, relationship with parents, self-concept, and some aspects of personal relationships, was completed by each woman and also by a close friend.

The replies showed that role innovation was significantly and positively related to having a mother who worked outside the home, as well as to the mother's own role innovation. Role innovators were also more inclined than the others to report feeling close to mother and less close to father, more likely to agree with mother's values and less likely to agree with father's; but less likely to say that their mother understood them. Lastly, they were more likely than the other women to agree with both parents as to college goals.

These same women were asked to describe themselves by giving ratings on a number of characteristics on 7-point scales. When asked to rate themselves as *masculine* versus *feminine*, the role innovators described themselves as less *feminine* but did not describe themselves as *masculine*. They agreed that they were 'concerned about feeling that you are always acting, never being true to yourself, or being yourself', and that they had thought about the questions, 'Who am I?', 'What do I want?', and 'What I will become?'. This would suggest their greater readiness to question accepted roles and behaviour for themselves.

Perhaps perceiving themselves to have unusual interests, in itself forced some self-examination. Interestingly, there was no relationship with self-perceived competence. But they did have as many romantic and platonic relationships with men as did the more traditional students.

It looks from this and other studies that parents' attitudes and roles are important. We might know more about the role of fathers if research workers had asked more sensible questions about the ways a father can facilitate his daughter's career – instead of chasing after 'deviance' and 'pathology'.

Several other pieces of research confirm the importance of mothers (see Tangri 1972 for a good review). Peterson (1958) and Klemmack and Edwards (1973) also found that women whose mothers worked were more likely to be career-oriented. Wasserman (1973) reports that significantly more women than men college students had mothers with degrees and postgraduate degrees. Douvan (1963) found that women who wanted supposedly 'masculine' occupational goals more often had working mothers.

Almquist and Angrist (1970) suggest one reason why the mother is important. They think that she acts as a 'role model' for her daughter. The daughter perhaps identifies with her mother's values. She sees that her mother gets satisfaction from work. And she has an example which she can imitate – demonstrating to her that it really is possible for a woman to have a role outside the home. Perhaps, too, families in which the mother works are more inclined to accept and value a woman's abilities.

This highlights a special problem for women who might want a career: the 'traditional' family does not provide them with adequate 'role models'. It is not surprising that more of the career-committed, in Almquist and Angrist's study, thought that their work choice was influenced by college professors or someone in the job. They were the lucky ones. Neither the media, nor public life, give most women much help here.

Even college teaching staff have few women in high status jobs or influential administrative positions. Fewer still combine career with family as most college women seem to want. Where else are students to get the evidence that women are capable of high level work? That they can find it satisfying? Or that it is acceptable for them to do so? Where else can they find out how to cope with a family and a career?

One point in passing concerning the view that women who take their careers seriously must be the product of disturbed family backgrounds and relationships. Why should this not be turned on its head? The question then becomes, 'what is wrong with the supposedly normal family, that it turns out so many women whose self-concepts so inhibit them from personal fulfilment?' Perhaps we should be thankful for deviance – if that is what it is. But 'deviance' has a high cost to the woman.

What do college women think men think?

Hawley (1971) points out that several studies have shown that women seem to make career choices that they think men will tolerate. Her study of older women showed that women's perception of male views of the feminine ideal varied according to the career group to which they belonged. Women in traditionally feminine occupations tended to think that men view behaviour in a sex-linked way, as appropriately male or female.

In view of the stereotypes which have been shown to be prevalent among male as well as female college students, it would be useful to know how they are influenced by what they think men think. Especially as the college men are presumably their potential husbands. It may be that the women are more influenced by male views than *vice versa* since the women are under more pressure to see marriage as their primary goal in life.

Tangri (1972), in the study mentioned above, asked the women students who had influenced their occupational choices. She came to the conclusion that faculty and female college friends may provide support for the role innovators. But a supportive boyfriend may be even more important. This is suggested by the finding that there was a relationship between role innovation and the views on sex roles held by the women's male friends. These women were more likely than other women to have boyfriends with less sex-typed views of women.

Rapoport, Payne, and Steinmann (1970) compared forty-five married with forty-five unmarried women college students. They studied their perceptions of themselves, their ideal woman, and their perceptions of men's ideal woman. The same students completed an inventory of attitudes to women's activities and satisfactions. There was no significant difference between the married and the single in what they thought men's ideal woman would be like. Both groups thought that most men would desire a woman whose activities, values, and satisfactions were mainly home-centred. They thought the men's own ideas would be considerably more extreme in this respect than they perceived themselves to be, or than they wished ideally to be. The married women, interestingly, saw themselves and the ideal selves as more 'self-achieving' than did the single women. The authors suggest that the married women, having secured a husband and stayed on at college, may have felt less influenced by traditional stereotypes.

Rossi (1965b) presented women with a list of typically 'male' professions – architect, business executive, college professor, doctor, engineer, lawyer, research scientist – and asked them to say which they themselves disapproved of for women, and which jobs were disapproved of by others. Sixty-eight per cent of the women said that they themselves did not disapprove. Sixty-five per cent thought that their mothers would not disapprove. Sixty per cent thought their fathers would not disapprove and 59 per cent thought that 'most women of their age and education' would not disapprove. The *husband* or *closest male friend* was least likely to be seen as tolerant; 50 per cent thought these men would disapprove. One third thought that most men of their age and education would definitely disapprove. Rossi suggests that the women may have been correct in thinking that fathers would be more tolerant than husbands of 'odd' professions for women. The fathers would not have to deal with the practical consequences, such as adjustments in their personal and family lives.

A study by the American National Opinion Research Centre (Miller 1963) asked women college graduates why they thought women are under-represented in medicine, engineering, and science. For medicine and science, the most frequent reasons given were that, 'A job in this field is too difficult for a woman to combine with family responsibilities', and that women in general want occasional or part-time work. Very few thought that women lack the skills. For engineering, the most frequent reasons chosen were that, 'Women are afraid they will be considered unfeminine if they enter these fields', and that parents discourage it. Twenty-four per cent thought that women lack the necessary skills.

Rossi suggests that the obstacles to women entering engineering operate earlier in life. They take the form of parental stereotypes concerning little girls' basic abilities, and 'feminine' behaviours. Obstacles to a career in maths and science come into operation when the women are older. They have more to do with the practical problems that they see in combining career and family.

Two final thoughts. It is quite possible that women attribute to men more stereotyped attitudes than the men themselves claim (see, for example, Steinmann and Fox 1966). Nonetheless, the women are right in thinking that the men's practical behaviour, and their sex-role stereotypes for women, will not give them much help in their careers. For example, the National Opinion Research Centre (Miller 1963) reports that college men were much more likely than women to believe that women should not choose a career difficult to combine with child-rearing, and that women should not work when the children are small. And they were between two and three times more likely to say that there was 'no need at all' for increased child-care facilities, equal opportunity in hiring and promotion, and encouragement of women to enter professions and national political office. Apparently, the men do not want to make the alterations in their personal and working lives which would permit women to have careers, nor do they want to see the State intervene to the same end. It is one thing to subscribe to the theoretical view that women are in some abstract way 'equal', and quite another to take half shares in housework, nappies, and childcare, or to relinquish the power and status of being the main 'breadwinner'. As Rossi (1965b) says, most women perceive this correctly, and most do what they say their future husbands prefer.

SIX

Women and their self-esteem

It is often said that women have lower self-esteem than men (see, for example, Bardwick 1971). This has been suggested as one reason why fewer women attempt high level academic work, or seek demanding and high status jobs (for example, O'Leary 1974). It has also been used to explain why more women suffer from depression and neurotic symptoms (see Chesler 1972). So it is important to know whether women really do undervalue themselves.

It would hardly be surprising if they did. Until very recently in Western countries, women were widely treated as inferior in law, politics, religion, and education as well as in society generally. Many of these discriminations remain. We have seen in Chapter 5 that there is evidence to suggest that college students still think that the average woman has fewer good qualities than the average man. Are women influenced by these beliefs when they evaluate themselves?

It need not necessarily be so. A woman could have a low

opinion of most other women, but see herself personally as different and superior to the rest. Alternatively, she might think that women, including herself, are inferior creatures – but think well of herself because she does as well as can be expected within her supposed limitations.

The research on sex differences in self-esteem is almost entirely restricted to children, adolescents, and college students. In their review of the findings up to 1974, Maccoby and Jacklin (1975) came to the conclusion that 'The similarity of the two sexes in self-esteem is remarkably uniform across age levels through college age' (Maccoby and Jacklin 1975:153). This means that some studies have demonstrated that women have higher levels of self-esteem than men, some have found no difference, and some found men to be higher.

Can we say, then, that there are no differences between the sexes in their opinions of their worth? Hardly. There are reasons for being cautious about how we interpret the evidence reviewed by Maccoby and Jacklin. One is that most studies of adult men and women have looked at a particular social group – college students. Another is that they tell us little about what qualities are seen as important by the two sexes. Two people can have equally high or low opinions of themselves, but for very different reasons. And their behaviour in any particular situation may depend on the particular kinds of qualities they think they possess. For example, Webster and Sobieszek (1974) reviewed some of the research on self-esteem and came to the conclusion that

'... one of the consequences of a high self-evaluation may be an increased willingness to perform in the future, and by extension, that a consequence of a low self-evaluation may be a decreased willingness to perform.

A second consequence of a high self-evaluation that appeared in several studies is a greater willingness to evaluate one's own future performances positively and a greater willingness to rank oneself highly within the group.'

(Webster and Sobieszek 1974:29)

Variation in Self-Esteem with Culture and Social Position

We have already seen in Chapter 3 that women and men in different cultures perceive and evaluate women differently. Could it be that women's and men's evaluations of *themselves* are also influenced by their social group – by class, culture, or subculture? Or by their particular social position within their group? A woman approaching middle-age, who values herself only as a mother, might find when her children leave home, that she has nothing to value herself for at all. Whereas a very similar woman in a close-knit community, might be in constant demand for advice and help from her married daughters – and feel more important than ever.

Kaplan (1973) was interested in the effects of age, sex, and social class on self-esteem. He predicted that self-esteem would not depend on age, or sex, or class alone, but that it would be influenced by interactions between these three variables. He interviewed 500 people, a representative sample of adults in Harris County, Texas. They completed a measure of what he called 'self-derogation', by which he meant the tendency to hold oneself in low esteem. One example of the items in his questionnaire, on which the individual rates her agreement or disagreement on a 4-point scale, is 'I feel that I am a person of worth, at least on an equal plane with others'. Disagreement with this item would count as 'self-derogation'. Another such item is 'At times I think I am no good at all'.

As he predicted, there were no overall sex differences in self-derogation when he looked at the sample as a whole. But there were in fact sex differences in certain subgroups within the sample. Among the less educated, white women held a poorer view of themselves than did the men. As many as 64 per cent of the white women with less than college education had high self-derogation scores, whereas 46 per cent of the men had high scores. Among college educated white people, it was the other way about. Thirty three per cent of white women with at least some college education had high self-derogation scores, as compared to 46 per cent of the men. Thus the more educated the woman, the better her view of herself. Better educated black women also had lower self-derogation scores than the less educated, but the differences were not statistically significant. In contrast, the few college educated black men in the sample had very high self-derogation scores indeed. So also did white men between the ages of fifty and fifty-nine years of age.

Conclusions from this study have to be tentative. The categories used to define social position are broad and crude. Some of the subgroups are very small (especially for black people). And the measure itself is a very global one. Nonetheless, the results do make some sense. We know that college educated men and women tend to favour more equal roles for the two sexes (see Chapter 2). And more educated women get better jobs and earn more. So it is not surprising if they do have a higher opinion of themselves. The older men are approaching retirement – and work is an important source of status for a man. Lastly, it is easy to speculate that college educated black men face many very special problems.

It would be nice to know more about the effects of a woman's particular social world on her self-esteem. We should be surprised if all working-class women thought badly of themselves. That this is indeed not the case, is suggested by Feldman and Feldman (1973) and Bendo and Feldman (1973). They found that even among women living on welfare, there were sharply contrasting attitudes to the role of women, and to their own capabilities. It would also be interesting to have some information on the effects of growing older, and changes in a woman's role over a lifetime. But what Kaplan's study (1973) does suggest is that almost all the research on self-esteem in adults has been done with people who are *least* likely to show sex differences favouring men – namely college students.

Sources of self-esteem

American college students do not differ in their level of self-esteem, but they do think that men have, and ought to have, more qualities to do with competence, self-assertion, and achievement. And they do think that women have, and ought to have, more warmth and expressiveness. They also still tend to think that women and men should have different roles in later life – with women putting home and family before academic achievement and work.

Since women are seen as different from men in these respects and are assessed by different standards, this suggests the hypothesis that women use different criteria from men when they evaluate themselves. It could be that women tend to undervalue themselves in some ways, without this leading to a lower opinion of themselves overall. Another possibility is that having certain qualities – such as competence and aggressiveness – would make a man think highly of himself; whereas a woman who possesses those same qualities would discount them, or even think worse of herself because of them. We shall come back to this issue later.

(a) *Social self-esteem*. First, however, we shall consider a different hypothesis – that there are some ways in which women actually have a better opinion of themselves than men do. Maccoby and Jacklin (1975) suggest, cautiously, that there may be a 'female cluster' of areas in which women are more confident.

As the authors point out, there certainly is some evidence that women describe themselves differently from men. Carlson (1970) discusses a series of studies which explore the hypothesis that the basic difference between male and female self-concepts is that men define themselves in 'individualistic' terms, whereas women define themselves in 'interpersonal' terms. That is, women define themselves by their relationships with other people. One of the measures used was the Carlson Adjective Check List. It is intended to assess the extent to which a person sees her or himself as individually or interpersonally oriented. From a list of thirty adjectives, each person chooses ten which apply to him or herself, and indicates which five are most self-descriptive. Fifteen of the thirty adjectives describe qualities which Carlson thinks are 'social'. That is, they are terms 'requiring an implicit social object'. The items defined as social are: attractive, generous, compassionate, considerate, co-operative, dependable, frank, friendly, leader, likeable, persuasive, sincere, sympathetic, tactful, and warm. The other fifteen adjectives Carlson categorizes as 'personal'. They are: ambitious, confident, creative, efficient, energetic, fair-minded, idealistic, imaginative, independent, optimistic, practical, rational, reasonable, versatile, and wise. People are classified as 'socially' oriented if they use more 'social' than 'personal' adjectives to describe themselves.

Carlson and Levy (1968) gave this questionnaire to eighty-eight men and seventy-five women, aged from eighteen to forty-five years. The men described themselves as significantly more 'personally' oriented than the women. The women described themselves as significantly more 'socially' oriented than the men, as was predicted.

Two other studies, with late adolescents, also find women to be more socially oriented (Carlson 1965; Carlson 1971). It is less clear whether there are such differences in younger children (see Maccoby and Jacklin 1975:159). Carlson (1970) summarizes her view thus: 'While the level of self-esteem remains constant and comparable for boys and girls, the basis of self-evaluation shifts dramatically, with males emphasising individualistic and females interpersonal definitions of the self' (Carlson 1970:265).

How far are these conclusions justified? It does look as if white American adult women describe themselves in more 'interpersonal' terms, according to Carlson's definition. But these studies do not tell us whether they also thought better of themselves for possessing these qualities. However, many of the 'social' items on the Adjective Check List look remarkably like the socially desirable qualities which American college students ascribe to 'women in general'. And many of the 'personal' or 'individualistic' items resemble the socially desirable qualities attributed to 'men in general'. So perhaps we can speculate that men think men ought to be ambitious, confident, efficient, and so forth, and tend to think men in general are so; they see themselves as being like this, and they value themselves for it. Women, on the other hand, think women should be compassionate, tactful, warm, and so forth; they see other women and themselves in these terms, and value themselves for it.

A study by McDonald (1968) fits in with this idea. He asked 528 seventeen-year-olds to fill out an Interpersonal Check List of 128 items. They had to rate themselves, their ideal selves, and their parents. On the basis of their replies, each person received a score for what he called 'Dominance' and a score for what he called 'Love'. By 'Dominance' he meant 'assertive, aggressive, leadership qualities'. By 'Love', he meant 'friendly, warm, co-operative characteristics'. Again, 'Dominance' resembles, on the face of it, Carlson's 'personal' orientation and the male stereotype. And 'Love' resembles the 'social' orientation and the female stereotype. McDonald did indeed find that the men described themselves as significantly higher on 'Dominance' and the women described themselves as significantly higher on 'Love'. And the women also wanted, ideally, to be higher on 'Love' than did the men.

How general is the social orientation of women? In McDonald's study, mentioned above, black men described themselves as higher in 'Love' than white men; whereas black and white women did not differ. Carlson and Levy, in their study of black American students (1970) did not find the women more socially oriented either; nor did Smart and Smart (1970), in a study of Asian–Indian students. So, like the stereotypes, women's self-images may vary with the culture, according to the roles they have within that culture.

(b) *Self-esteem and achievement*. We shall now look at the other side of the coin – the ways in which women may think less of themselves.

College women think they are as intelligent as men. In a survey of 171,509 American college students, the two sexes rated themselves very similarly on academic ability (Wasserman 1973). This is an accurate assessment since men and women undergraduates get very similar grades. Unfortunately we have no evidence on how women other than college students evaluate their intelligence. However, we do know that women are less confident about predicting what grade they will get, and less confident on many tasks, even when objectively they do as well as men. They also see themselves as less powerful – and not only physically (see Maccoby and Jacklin 1975 for a review of this evidence). In addition, there is a tendency for college women to attribute their achievements to luck, or to some other factor outside their own control. Whereas college men are likely to see their achievements as due to their own skill and effort. But one study found that, among college students, feminists were an exception to this generalization about women; they were more likely to have a feeling of personal control over their lives (Sanger and Alker 1972).

It seems that, despite seeing themselves as equally intelligent, women consider themselves less capable of doing well academically and in many tasks. This could be because they think they are relatively lacking in other qualities necessary for success – such as assertiveness, independence, and competence. But there may be more to it than this. Could it be that the meaning success has for women is in some way different from the meaning it has for men?

Early research on 'achievement motivation' concentrated mainly on men. One common way in which researchers have tried to measure how much people want to achieve, is to look at their fantasies. This is done by means of projective tests. In a typical study using the Thematic Apperception Test, the person is presented with a rather ambiguous picture of people doing something, and asked to tell a story about it. The story is then analysed and the person receives a score for 'achievement motivation', which depends on the extent to which the stories are concerned with achievement. The assumption is that the person 'projects' his own wishes and fears into the story he tells.

Early research showed that among men, a person's score on this type of measure predicts his achievement behaviour; when placed in competitive situations, their achievement scores on projective tests rose. However, when women were presented with the same type of measure, the results were puzzling and inconsistent. In many studies, there was no correlation between the amount of achievement imagery that a woman showed on the tests and her performance in academic and test situations. Nor did the measures predict how hard she would strive to succeed. And when women were placed in competitive situations, they often showed no increase in achievement imagery.

This is a complicated matter and a good deal of research has been devoted to it. Those interested in reading more about studies of achievement motivation and behaviour in women, and about the various theories that have been put forward, should consult the reviews by Stein and Bailey (1973), O'Leary

(1974), and Maccoby and Jacklin (1975). Here we are concerned with women's own views of their achievement.

There are several possible explanations for the seemingly inconclusive results. It might be that women are simply less interested in achievement for its own sake, and only value it when it leads to something they do value, such as social approval or affection from others (Crandall 1963). However, Stein and Bailey (1973), in their review of the literature, come to the conclusion that women do want to achieve and be successful. For example, Veroff, Wilcox, and Atkinson (1953) found that, in non-competitive situations, schoolgirls actually produced more achievement imagery than boys in their responses to projective tests. But, unlike boys, their scores did not rise in response to competition. Another complication was that they produced their achievement fantasies in responses to the male and not female pictures.

If women do have achievement fantasies, why do situations which increase men's achievement scores, not influence women to raise their scores too? Stein and Bailey (1973) suggest that women do not want the same kinds of achievements as men. They think that women want to achieve in interpersonal relationships and social skills and are less interested in academic success. And they go on to argue that this is because social success is culturally defined as appropriate for a woman, whereas academic success and competence are not. There is indeed some support for this view. For example, French and Lesser (1964) found that college women who valued 'traditional' women's roles, did increase achievement imagery after they were told that they would be asked to do a 'test of social skills' which would predict how successful they were likely to be socially and in their marriages.

(c) *Women and fear of success*. Horner (1968, 1970, and 1972) offers a different kind of explanation. Her view is that many women do want to achieve, but they are also afraid of success, because they see it as having negative consequences for them. She called this 'Motive to Avoid Success' or 'Fear of Success'.

In order to test this hypothesis, she used a verbal projective test. She asked ninety women college students to complete a story which began 'At the end of first term finals, Anne finds herself at the top of her medical school class . . .' She also asked eighty-eight male college students to complete a story beginning with a sentence which was identical except for the fact that the name John was substituted for the name Anne. She then examined the stories for signs of 'fear of success'.

She considered fear of success to be present if the story contained statements showing 'conflict about the success, the presence or anticipation of negative consequences because of the success, denial of effort or responsibility for attaining the success, denial of the cue itself, or some other bizarre or inappropriate response to the cue' (Horner 1972:162). She found that fifty-nine of the ninety women wrote stories containing themes showing avoidance or fear of success, whereas only eight of the eighty-eight men did. An example she considers typical is one in which 'Anne deliberately lowers her academic standing the next term and does all she subtly can to help Carl, whose grades come up. She soon drops out of med-school, they marry, and Carl goes on in school while she raises their family' (Horner 1972:162). Other women saw Anne as unhappy, aggressive, and unmarried. Horner comments that in general 'Unusual excellence in women was clearly associated for them with the loss of femininity, social rejection, personal or societal destruction, or some combination of the above' (Horner 1972:162). The men, on the other hand, describe John as straightforwardly pleased with his success, and as going on to a successful career.

Horner interpreted her results to mean that the women were projecting their own anxieties and conflicts about success on to Anne. In support of this, she found that women who were low in fear of success on her measure, behaved more like men in competitive situations – that is, they performed better in competition; whereas women who were high on fear of success performed better in non-competitive situations. She suggests that the amount of fear of success that a woman shows may partly depend on her ability, and on how much she wants to achieve. A woman who has no strong desire for achievement would not be expected to fear success.

Feather and Raphelson (1974) put forward a rather different

interpretation. Perhaps the women's stories simply show sex-role stereotyping rather than fear of success. That is, they reflect the popular belief that academic success is inappropriate and undesirable for women. They point out that stories using Horner's technique never asked men to write stories about women, or women to write stories about men. If their hypothesis is correct, then men should write stories describing negative consequences following from women's achievements, while women should not express fear of success themes when writing about men.

To test this they studied 126 male and eighty-eight female Australian students, and eighty-three male and 113 female American students. Half the men and half the women wrote stories in response to the male cue. The rest of the men and women wrote stories in response to the female cue.

They found, as predicted, that men from both countries wrote significantly more fear of success stories to the Anne cue than they did to the John cue. But the women differed. In the Australian group, the women also wrote significantly more fear of success stories to the Anne cue than to the John cue. However, for the American women, there was no important difference between the proportion of fear of success stories written to the two different cues. Both American and Australian men actually wrote more fear of success stories to the Anne cue than did the women, though the difference was only significant for the American sample.

Feather and Raphelson conclude that the Australian results clearly support their hypothesis. Australian men and women agreed that Anne's success is more likely to have negative consequences than John's. This certainly looks like sex-role stereotyping. However, the American results are not so clear-cut. The men tend to see more negative consequences following from Anne's success than from John's, whereas the women do not. This contrasts with Horner's original findings. One possible explanation offered by Feather and Raphelson is that the American students in this study differ from Horner's in their sex-role attitudes, perhaps because they have different family and/or socio-economic backgrounds.

The discrepancy between the American and the Australian

students could reflect cultural differences in terms of the strength of sex-role stereotyping – and perhaps also the impact of the women's movement in America in recent years. The sex-role stereotype hypothesis is not incompatible with the fear of success hypothesis, as Feather and Raphelson point out. It could be that women fear success precisely because they are strongly aware that other people see academic and work achievement as undesirable for women.

There are other reasons for being cautious about the conclusions we come to about this type of research. Tresemer (1973) points out that there has been a great deal of research along the lines of Horner's studies, and the results have been variable and sometimes contradictory. He reviewed forty-six studies, many of them unpublished, and found that the proportion of women writing fear of success stories ranged from 11 per cent to 88 per cent. This could be partly because the method of scoring used in the studies is vague and ambiguous. For what one research worker considers to show fear of success is scored by another as fear of failure, or anxiety, or whatever.

Another problem is that many studies find men showing as much fear of success as women. Tresemer reviewed twenty-two studies in which men as well as women were included and found that the proportion of men writing fear of success stories to the male cue ranged from 22 per cent to 88 per cent – rather similar to the results for women. However, it may be that there are important differences in the kind of negative consequences that they expect from success. Some clues about this come from a study by Hoffman (1974a). She analysed the fear of success stories told by a group of college men and women. She found that the women most commonly told stories in which Anne suffered social rejection as a result of her success. For example, one said: 'She has no social life and therefore has spent all first semester studying. She was always a good student. Lonely but good.' Forty-two per cent of the women's fear of success stories contained this type of theme. Whereas only 15 per cent of the men's stories did. By contrast, the most common theme among the men was one in which the whole value of the achievement was questioned. Thirty per cent of the men's stories contained this theme, as compared with only 15 per cent of the women's.

For example, in the story, John 'graduates with honors and hates being a doctor. He wonders what it was all for.'

Comments

The difference in the ways that men and women value themselves fits in very well with their notions of the different life roles expected of them. But which comes first? Very likely this is not a sensible question. Girls and women learn at one and the same time, that they are supposed to have certain qualities, that this is what is expected of wives and mothers, and that wives and mothers they are going to be. All this would be fine and good. But they also learn that they are not supposed to have qualities which belong to roles they are not intended to have. Without these qualities they are disabled in academic and working life. Yet when they do possess them, they experience conflict and anxiety.

However, there is another side to this: Hollender (1972) suggests that:

'The maintenance of high social self-esteem for males is probably contingent on continued success in meeting cultural standards of masculine achievement. Since cultural standards shift and change with advancing age, a certain amount of conformity is required of males as they change their behaviour to meet new cultural standards.'   (Hollender 1972:346)

He found that male college students who had high self-esteem also had a high need for approval. He suggests that the 'individualistic' masculine orientation described by Carlson (1970), shows actual conformity to culturally approved male roles and the requirements of this are pretty exacting. 'Masculinity' also has its price.

SEVEN

Women's perceptions of themselves

Would you describe yourself as generally satisfied or unsatisfied with life, or neither, particularly?

'Generally satisfied. Well, I mean to say *you have to make the best of things*.' (Painter and decorator's wife.)

'I don't really know. Satisfied, I suppose. I suppose I have to be. What's the point of being any other way when *you know you've got to be satisfied*.' (Factory hand's wife.)

(Oakley 1974b:68)

In Chapters 1 and 2, we discussed some popular views of what women's roles ought to be. But it was argued that 'ought' and 'want' are not necessarily the same thing. Living out a role day by day may be very different, be it better or worse, from what one imagined.

What do women think of the roles that they wind up with? How satisfied are they with marriage or singlehood? With parenthood or childlessness? With working or staying at home?

How does experience of these roles affect the way women see themselves? And how does the picture change over the course of a lifetime?

Such questions cannot have simple answers. For any individual woman, the meaning of the roles she has, and her satisfaction with them, may be influenced by a whole host of other factors. For example, the effects of work will obviously depend partly on the nature of the job itself; whether she finds it interesting, whether it is well paid or poorly paid, and so on. Her views on one role may also depend on her other roles; whether she is married, has children, whether her husband wants her to work, how much help she gets with housework. Her own initial preferences and views on women's roles are also important; for instance, whether she feels guilty about working, and whether she works from choice or necessity.

'Satisfaction' is itself a complex notion. Events such as marriage, or the arrival of a baby, may have a multitude of consequences. A baby or small toddler may be delightful to its parents in many ways – but also wreak havoc with their sleep, their sex-life, their social life, and their bank balance. What answer are they then supposed to give a researcher who baldly asks whether the child has made them happier? Both 'yes' and 'no' are true in some ways and not in others. Can they really take a statistical mean for their overall satisfaction? More detailed questioning may bring an answer which contradicts the initial one, or it may uncover feelings which are mixed and contradictory.

Apart from this, as Rossi (1972) has pointed out, people are often less willing to express ambivalent or negative feelings about roles which feel 'obligatory' than about roles which feel 'optional'. It may be difficult for women to admit to themselves as well as to others, that they are in some ways dissatisfied with marriage and motherhood, since these are the roles they are supposed to want first and foremost. It is much easier to own up to dissatisfactions with work, for instance. This may sometimes lead people to say they are satisfied when they are not. But perhaps a more common situation is one in which they happily describe rewards which they genuinely do feel, and leave out of the picture, or 'play down', the frustrations which are also genuinely felt.

Research on satisfactions is rather fragmented. There is an enormous literature on patterns of sex-role relationships within the family; on relationships with kin; on the effects of women working; on division of labour within the home; and on children; but there is a good deal less on the woman's own view of herself and her life. What there is focuses mainly on her traditional, family roles and on the effects of the supposedly 'new' and 'deviant' role on the traditional ones. Thus there is, for instance, much more on what women feel about their marriages, than on what they feel about their work.

What follows is a brief look at some scattered evidence. It is not a unified, nor a complete picture. Since we have seen, in Chapter 2, that most people see marriage and motherhood as women's primary roles, we shall look at these first, followed by a look at work, and at some of the ways of integrating the two.

Marital satisfaction and the effects of marriage on the self-concept

Marriage is increasingly popular. At the present time, the proportion of married people in the population is greater than it was at the beginning of the century. People are getting married younger. True, they divorce more often, but a large percentage of divorced people marry again (Bernard 1973:19, 121–9).

Yet we know extraordinarily little about the effects of marriage on women's personalities and on their views of themselves. Bernard (1973), reviewing some of the literature, came to the conclusion that although marriage is usually thought to be bad for men and good for women, in fact it is the other way round. Wives compare poorly with men, and with single women, in terms of general satisfaction with life, marriage, and mental and physical health. Yet, when women are asked whether they are satisfied with their marriages, they tend to say 'yes'. How can these two observations be reconciled? Are women influenced by the belief that they must be happy, since they are supposed to be? Perhaps they have the difficulty that, when faced with questions about satisfaction, they find marriage has advantages and disadvantages, and the disadvantages are more difficult to admit to. Perhaps they do not attribute the problems and frustrations they find in marriage to the institution of marriage itself, but to some other factor, such as their own failings.

One has to be careful about the evidence here. It could be that initial differences in background, personality, or some other factor, influence marriage prospects. So that women who are going to get married differ from women who are going to remain single, even before the marriage takes place. It is more difficult to explain the difference between married women and married men (but see Bernard 1973 : 35–9).

The evidence on marital satisfaction tells us a little about what women like and dislike in marriage. On the whole, the surprising finding is that the husband–wife relationship itself has a rather low priority. Lopata (1971), for example, asked women to mention the satisfactions of the homemaker role. Most of these women had chosen to put the homemaker role first in their lives, yet only 9 per cent spontaneously referred to husbands as one of the satisfactions.

It would be more interesting to know which women, in which circumstances, are satisfied with what. It would also be interesting to know how women's self-images change, following marriage, and in the course of their marriages. We can find no study which looks at this. The sort of information we have got is that college-educated women in some way structure or adapt their personalities and self-images, in *anticipation* of marriage. This is suggested by the literature on fear of success and sex roles (see Chapters 5 and 6). Both husbands and wives agree that wives make more personal adjustments in marriage than do husbands (Burgess and Wallin 1953). There is also evidence that single career women describe themselves differently from married career women (Fogarty, Rapoport, and Rapoport 1971) and housewives (Rossi 1965a), but this could well be due to self-selection into and out of marriage, rather than the effects of marriage itself.

Being a mother

Much of what has been said about the research on marriage also applies to motherhood. There are similar contradictions between studies, and similar difficulties in interpreting the results. On the one hand, mothers often do say that children are a source of satisfaction: for instance, in Lopata's study of American house-wives (see above), 38 per cent of the women mentioned children as being one of the satisfactions of the homemaker role. This was by far the most common response, taking precedence over other aspects of the family relationships, over housework, and over the relationship with the husband. When Rainwater, Coleman, and Handel (1959) asked American working-class wives 'What is the best thing that ever happened to you?' a large proportion said that it was having a baby (Rainwater, Coleman, and Handel 1959:88).

On the other hand, when 217 mothers in Detroit were asked 'How is a woman's life changed by having children?', the most common reply was that children restricted her freedom, and only half gave replies that could be considered in any way positive (Hoffman 1974b:48). (There was, incidentally, no differ-ence between working and non-working mothers in the fre-quency of positive and negative replies.)

Bernard (1973) has even argued that research evidence so far suggests that children do not either, initially, or when they are older, make women generally happier. If anything they make them less happy. One study (Veroff and Feld 1970) compared mothers with childless women. Although about half in each group described themselves as 'very happy', the mothers were more likely than the childless women to say that they found marriage 'restrictive', that they had 'problems in marriage' and that they were less satisfied with the marital relationship. There were no differences between the two groups as to whether they felt inadequate or dissatisfied with themselves.

However, global comparisons between mothers and childless women are misleading. Childless women are unusual, and may differ from mothers in their initial goals and preferences and in their other life experiences.

Relevant here are studies of couples who wish for children,

but are unable to have them. Humphrey (1975) points out that 'Anyone whose concept of marriage was derived entirely from fiction might be led to suppose that fertility was a sine qua non of marital happiness' (Humphrey 1975). Yet his review of several pieces of research suggests that the reality is rather different: childlessness does not necessarily make a marriage less happy in the long term, and may even lead to greater closeness and affection between husband and wife. Indeed, when Humphrey himself studied forty infertile couples who adopted children, he found no more marital problems among the childless, and more sexual maladjustment among the adopters (Humphrey 1969).

Humphrey (1975) conducted a repertory grid investigation of the meaning of parenthood, and came to the perhaps not astonishing conclusion that it was rather different for women and men. 'Contentment and motherliness were more strongly associated in the minds of wives than contentment and fatherliness in the minds of husbands' (Humphrey 1975). The men associated fatherhood with masculinity; whereas neither parents nor childless couples saw femininity and motherhood as related to each other.

A different way of investigating the effects of children is to look at women's satisfaction at different stages in a marriage. Rollins and Feldman (1970) found that overall satisfaction with life and marriage tended to be highest for women who did not yet have children, very much lower for women with small children, remaining low until well after the children had grown up and left home. There is some disagreement between researchers as to whether marital satisfaction does indeed rise again in late life (Rollins and Cannon 1974; Spanier, Lewis, and Cole 1975; Ryder 1973).

Note that the measures used in the Rollins and Feldman study do not refer to children directly. The mothers in this study might well have said, if asked, that children brought them happiness. The criterion is a complex one, and many other factors unrelated to children may have influenced these women's relative satisfaction with marriage over the years. There are no comparative data for childless women at different stages of their marriages.

Apart from this, the information provided by this sort of study is rather limited, it shows broad general trends but says little about the circumstances in which children may contribute to, or detract from, happiness and satisfaction. Statistical averages mask the complex processes which may be very different from one couple to another. Lopata (1971), for instance, has suggested that less educated wives may feel that children bring them closer to their husbands, whereas better educated wives, who may already have a closer relationship with their husbands, feel that children drive them apart. Brown, Bhrolchain, and Harris (1975) found that the working-class mothers of young children in their Camberwell study were faced with more problems, were more physically restricted and isolated because of their children, and had less access to help than did middle-class mothers. It is a truism and a fact to say that the effects on a woman of having children depend on the circumstances in which she brings them up.

Apart from being 'satisfied' or 'dissatisfied', how else does motherhood affect women? Some of the effects on women of childbirth itself are discussed in Chapter 9. But of the effects of growing children and the changing nature of the maternal role we know very little. It seems likely that they depend a good deal on the sex-role attitudes of the particular woman and her social group.

This brings us to the question of how women's views of themselves change as they grow older and as their roles change.

Growing older

The stereotypical image of women focuses on the youngish married woman with children. So does most of the research. Yet even mothers cannot make motherhood the centre of their lives indefinitely. What happens when the children leave home?

Women whose identity does not revolve solely round the family can become free to develop other aspects of themselves, as their children grow more independent. Women who are committed to their careers often see the years when the children are small as a 'phase', during which they must temporarily work part-time or give up work, but after which they look forward to returning to their jobs (Fogarty, Rapoport, and Rapoport 1971).

But for women for whom motherhood is the only important role in life, then, Bart (1969, 1971) suggests, losing this role means that they see themselves as having little value, and may even develop a serious depression. She argues that in Western child-centred societies, a woman's status drops in middle age and after, so that not only do older women think less of themselves, but they are also less valued by others. Even the role of 'grandmother' was seen as pretty unimportant by the housewives whom Lopata interviewed (see Chapter 2).

Sandsberg (1976) discusses the use of grid technique in relation to interviewing fifteen middle-aged women. She gives several interesting single case examples. For instance, one woman used the construct *realistic-dreaming*; when it was pointed out that she had characterized herself as a dreamer, she became embarrassed, since being a dreamer is most often applied to the young. Of great importance for all the women was the construct *secure–insecure*. Sandsberg thought that it was fear of losing feminine attractiveness that resulted in these feelings of insecurity. This would not be really surprising in a culture that, more than anything else, focuses on a female's looks. These are the things that get a man, keep him from going to other women, make him proud to be seen with one, and make him keep wanting to go to bed with her. If the woman feels her attractiveness is going – what has she to put in its place? In Kelly's sense (1955), it is going to lead to anxiety. For the woman is going to be confronted with a situation that has far less meaning for her than her present one.

Society gives no help to these women. There are no rituals, as there are in some societies, to indicate the entering into a new situation, and no rules to give guidance on how to give up old roles and take on new ones. It is far from surprising that many middle-aged women become depressed. Sandsberg (1976) gives the following excellent quote from a famous sculptor when asked if he had tried to make busts of middle-aged women.

'I've tried, but it is very difficult. Middle-age women seem to have no image. They hide behind make-up and sweet and youthful manners. They bind up their breasts, and try to hide

113

it if the hips are too wide. Sometimes, when they get lost in thought, one notices that they really are grandmothers.

The old woman is much more interesting. An old wrinkled face may be very beautiful. And the old woman possesses an image: the greatest artists have painted her.

Looking at her, one is reminded of The Grandmother, taking care of all the children that surround her.

Middle-aged woman is difficult, with lines in her face which she tries to hide. But most important: *she has no image.'*

(Sandsberg 1976)

Old age

The sculptor sees Grandmother as interesting. But for many people old age brings poverty, ill-health, and loneliness (Townsend 1963) and since women live longer, more women than men are in long-term hospital care for physical and mental diseases, and more face widowhood. How do old women see old age?

Lopata (1973) argues that widowhood, in particular, deprives a woman of one of her major roles. It poses a threat to her view of who she is. From a study of 300 American widows, she came to the conclusion that better educated women are more likely to deal with this threat by developing a new sense of their own identity. Presumably, educated women also tend to be better-off, and hence have more means at their disposal for making a new life.

Heyman (1970) points out that the husband's retirement may cause special problems for the wife. They have more time together than ever before, and there is often a good deal of uncertainty about what their respective roles should be. Stinnett, Collins, and Montegomery (1970) found that older wives were less satisfied with their marriages than were their husbands. But Heyman thinks that the wife's own retirement may be less difficult for her, because it is less abrupt a transition than it is for a man. In support of this, Townsend found that spinsters and women with no children complained more about retirement, but even so, they accepted it more easily than men did. Here is one widow's account of how it happened: '... my daughter said, "Mum, you've had to fight hard in your life and there's help for you. I think you want a rest, Mum, and you should give it up." I think my children were right, and I had had a hard life, and I gave it up.' One spinster said 'We found a lot to do here. When you get old you've got enough to do in the house. We've been spending what we've saved' (Townsend 1963:170).

Being a houseworker

As we said in Chapter 2, housework is a central aspect of women's traditional role, which is frequently undervalued or forgotten.

Oakley (1974a) was interested in the question of whether women liked housework and, if they did, then why did they and whether they identified themselves with this aspect of the 'women's role'. She interviewed forty mothers aged between twenty and thirty, selected on a random basis from two areas of London. Half of the women were working-class and half were middle-class (according to the Registrar-General's classification of their husbands' occupations).

Based on the responses to structured interviews, ratings were made of the women's satisfaction/dissatisfaction with housework, and life generally.

When they were asked the open-ended question, 'What would you say are the best things about being a housewife?' half the women mentioned 'being your own boss'. This was by far the most common response. It certainly contradicts the popular stereotype of women, and especially of housewives, as being passive and preferring the passive role. Nonetheless, Oakley suggests that the autonomy of the housewife is more theoretical than real, since they actually feel under an obligation to get the work done. As one woman put it: 'The worst thing is I suppose that you've got to do it because you are at home. Even though I've got the option of not doing it, I don't really feel I could not do it, because I feel I *ought* to do it' (Oakley 1974:44). Only one woman mentioned housework as one of the 'best things' about being a housewife. Fourteen mentioned housework as one of the worst things, and fourteen mentioned monotony, repetitiousness, and boredom. Different tasks were differently valued. For instance, ironing and washing-up were most unpopular, whereas shopping and cooking the most popular.

Despite the common claim, among sociologists and in the Press, that it is middle-class women who are dissatisfied with housework, while working-class women are not, there were no differences in this small study between the working-class and the middle-class, nor between the more and less educated, in the degree of satisfaction with housework. The majority of women from all classes were dissatisfied (twenty-eight of the forty were classified as 'dissatisfied' or 'very dissatisfied'). Oakley points out that the working-class women are more likely to say at the start that they like or 'don't mind' housework, but further questioning reveals a great deal of dissatisfaction; whereas middle-class women are more likely to start off by saying they do not like it. This is important, because a great many studies of women's satisfaction with their roles tend to use simple yes/no questions without exploring further. This may be one reason why previous studies have found class differences in satisfaction (for example, Komarovsky 1967; Rosser and Harris 1965).

There was disagreement about the housewife role. One woman said:

'I think of myself as a housewife, but I don't think of myself as a cabbage. A lot of people think that they're housewives and they're cabbages: I don't like to think I'm only a housewife ... I usually say "I'm a wife and a mother and I've got a part-time job." People look down on housewives these days.'
(Oakley 1974:48)

Another said: 'I would hate to think of myself as just being a housewife ...' (Oakley 1974a:74).

An assessment was made of identification with the housewife role. This was defined as 'a condition in which the responsibility for housework is felt as feminine, and therefore a personal attribute, normally as a result of childhood identification with the mother as role model' (Oakley 1974a:117). The rating was based on answers to several groups of questions. These were:

(1) A 'Ten Statements Test' of domestic role identity. The women were asked to write on a card ten answers to the question 'Who am I?' addressed to themselves.

(2) Further exploratory questions about the statements they had made.

(3) Open-ended questions, such as whether the person who brought them up (usually the mother) had worked, and why; whether she was working now; whether she was happy as a housewife; and what sort of housewife she was. They were then asked whether they had helped around the house when young, and if so, what they felt about it; and whether as teenagers they had wanted to be like their mothers, as regards getting married and having children, working when married, and training for a career. They were also asked about their parents' expectations for them concerning education, employment, marriage, and children. Finally, they were asked about their present relationship with their mothers.

From answers to the open-ended questions, 53 per cent of the women were rated as showing high identification with the housewife role, 43 per cent showed 'medium' identification, and 5 per cent showed low identification. There were no social class differences. The women also reported very similar childhood experiences as influencing their housework attitudes, tending to refer to their mothers and to their role about the house.

However, there were class differences in the statements that the women made about themselves in response to the ten statements test. The working-class women were much more likely to say 'I am a housewife' and to say it early on in the list. Seventeen of the twenty working-class women described themselves as 'housewives' as against eight of the twenty middle-class women.

The frequency with which the women described themselves as housewives could have been because this was an interview about housework, but this would not explain why there was a class difference, nor why more of the working-class women described domestic roles generally. The middle-class women, on the other hand, tended to give more self-descriptions involving personality descriptions and mood.

Why the discrepancy between the combined rating of identification with the role of housewife, and the answers to the ten statements test? Oakley suggests that they are tapping two different dimensions. The first measure taps internalized norms, which become a part of the person in such a way as to be automatically expressed in behaviour. The second measure asks for a verbal self-description. Whether or not internalized norms are referred to in statements about oneself may 'relate to the psycho-linguistic question of the extent to which self and (housewife) role are differentiated in the self-concept' (Oakley 1974a : 125). Following Bernstein (1971), she argues that the way we learn language, and the language we learn, varies in the extent to which it allows conceptual differentiation of self from role. Working-class women learn a 'language of implicit meaning' which tends to stress shared structure and identification (the ways in which they are like other people in the same role), rather than individual differences.

An additional finding relevant here was that middle-class women were slightly more likely to mention one or both of the wife and mother roles, without mentioning the housewife role at all, and they were more likely to mention other non-domestic roles, as well as political, religious, or ethnic affiliations. But the difference is marginal. Taking all the women together, only 4 per cent of responses mentioned roles outside the family. For most of the women then, it seems that the family roles were the ones considered 'core' roles, central to their idea of who they are.

Being a worker

Most women work for money. Single women work to support themselves, and married women who work do so to support their families or to improve the family standard of living. When Rosenfeld and Perella (1965) asked a national sample of married and single American women what was their most important reason for working, the most common response given was financial need. Yet the supposedly 'traditional' view of women's work is that it is a secondary role, at least for married women – at best an 'option' to be fitted around the needs of husband and children, at worst, an undesirable necessity justifiable only by the needs of the family.

Is this how all working women see themselves? Or do some

have a greater commitment and involvement in their jobs? Hoffman (1963) points out that women who say they are working 'for money' may in fact have a variety of different reasons for working. Indeed, women with children, who know that public opinion is against them, may not want to admit that they also like to work, for fear that someone might tell them they are neglecting their families or rejecting their children. 'Money' is an acceptable reason to give. It is most likely also a true one, but it is not the only one.

In support of this, Rosenfeld and Perella (1965) found that only one quarter of the women who said they worked from economic necessity actually said they would give up work if they were not in need. When Parnes *et al.* (1970) asked older married women whether they would work if they did not have to, about half said they would.

For mothers, in particular, the decision to work, and the choice of job, seldom depends on personal wishes alone. They are hedged round with practical considerations – such as the type of work available, looking after the children, fitting in with school hours, and getting the housework done. The background factors associated with women's employment, and the circumstances which help to make it possible, have been reviewed by Hoffman and Nye (1974). What does seem fairly clear is that, if they can get over the practical problems, many women, including mothers and wives, want something for themselves from their jobs, other than money.

What else, then, are they working for? In a national sample of American women, Sobol (1963) found that 21 per cent of the women said they worked 'to do something important', 'to have a career', because they 'liked the job', or for similar reasons. The better educated women were more likely to give this kind of reason, perhaps in part because they could get more attractive jobs. Rosenfeld and Perella (1965) also found that women whose children were older, were more likely than women with small children to say that 'personal satisfaction' was their most important reason for working. Presumably this is because most women with very young children work only if they have to, and as the children grow up, they are more free to please themselves.

Weiss and Samelson (1958) asked women what activities made them feel useful and important. Employed mothers mentioned some aspect of their job, more often than housework or family roles. This did not mean that they disliked being wives and mothers, for they mentioned those roles just as often as the women who were not employed. What it does seem to mean, is that the job contributed something extra, which they did not get at home.

What gives one woman personal satisfaction or a feeling of being important and useful may be infinitely boring and trivial to another. However, we know very little about what particular jobs mean to individual women.

It depends in part on local traditions and social context. Haller and Rosenmayr (1971) found that married women textile workers, in Austria, were often satisfied and highly committed to their work, despite the fact that it offered low pay and poor conditions. The explanation they suggest is that these women are often in isolated communities in which the work has become a tradition; and their social life, in and out of work, is with people in the same jobs. Moreover, women who recognize the similarities of their work outside the home to their roles within, are more likely to want to take jobs outside.

Deverson and Lindsay (1975), in a study of middle-class English women, came to the conclusion, that in wanting a paid job, they were mainly seeking a way out of boredom and loneliness. They comment that 'The advent of the part-time job has been a woman's salvation in this respect. To be a woman is fine, but to be just a woman is not enough' (Deverson and Lindsay 1975:110).

There are certain broad differences between men and women in the type of work that they choose, and in what they look for in a job. Garai and Scheinfeld (1968) reviewing this literature, conclude that men desire jobs which give power, profit, independence, and prestige; women look for interest, work with people, and work helping others. Men are more concerned with getting a steady job with opportunities for promotion, good pay, and substantial benefits. Women seek interesting work, fair supervision by friendly bosses, and congenial work and conditions.

These broad generalizations probably obscure more than they clarify, especially since women's work roles are changing. We have already discussed how women are encouraged to develop interests considered appropriate to the 'feminine role' – and working with people, and helping others, certainly seems to fit in there! Since they are not supposed to see work as a main role, and since their choice of work is often limited by the demands of home and family, it is hardly surprising if many women ask only for agreeable work situations.

Some of the factors which make college women choose careers which do not fit this pattern are discussed in Chapter 4. Working-class and less educated women do not have this kind of choice. But there is, quite simply, hardly any research in any depth which asks women how they see themselves as workers.

One study which did do this was by Holter (1970) in Oslo (see Chapter 2). One thousand 'blue-collar' and 'white-collar' employees of all ages and both sexes were interviewed. She found that, on the whole, the women tended to be less ambitious than the men about getting advancement and jobs which give some independence from supervision. She also found that the women were more likely to describe themselves as less confident in their own capacities at work, as leaning more on supervisors' authority, as feeling nervous in the presence of supervisors, as preferring a 'nice' to a 'capable' boss, and as being less in favour of technical changes at work. They were also less likely to identify with and feel concerned about the company.

It is important to realize here that these are broad differences only, and that on most of these questions, large numbers of women give similar responses to the men. Often the differences are very small. In particular, the percentages of women and men who think they are doing 'very well' at the present jobs, are actually very similar.

Other studies have suggested that, even if women sometimes have lower aspirations at work than men, they would still like more opportunities for promotion, responsibility, and independence, than they actually get (see Livingstone 1953;

Blomquist 1962; Marchak 1973). White (1973) has even suggested that women, rather than men, are the ones who consider autonomy at work an important factor in job satisfaction.

Holter also studied the relationship between sex-role norms and values, and behaviours at work. There was actually rather little association between the two among women (less than with the men). However, women with less traditional sex-role standards *did* have significantly higher aspirations; they less often reported losing emotional control at work, were less concerned about personal relationships and feelings, less likely to lean on authority, and more likely to be identified with the company. It did seem then that women who wanted more 'equal' sex-roles generally, considered themselves, as workers, more similar to men.

This is an interesting point. Several lines of evidence suggest there is a conflict for women at work, between 'being a woman' and 'being a worker'. This may be a particular problem for career-oriented women. Employers often think that professional and managerial jobs require qualities that women do not have (see, for example, Hartnett 1975; O'Leary 1974). At the same time, when women do show these qualities – such as ambition, self-assertion, aggression, competence, independence – they are condemned as 'unfeminine'. They are in a double-bind. But again, we lack evidence as to how successful career women resolve this dilemma.

Problems

Up until now, we have been talking rather as if 'roles' were like shoes: they come ready-made; you choose the ones you want or can get; you put them on – and you change into others when necessary.

But roles are not like shoes. Even in a traditional marriage, where both parties agree that the man is the breadwinner and 'a woman's place is in the home', there is room for disagreement about what this involves. He may think that a 'good husband' hands over his pay packet unopened. She may think that any 'real man' should make the important decisions about money. At this point, they have to negotiate some arrangement that both can accept. They may experiment with a solution that neither had thought of at first – such as planning the budget together Of course, the experiment may not work. In which case, they have to try another. In this sense, roles are lived.

Living a role requires a great deal of experimenting and inventiveness. It also means continual negotiation with others in trying to understand how they see things and trying to change their views or behaviour – or one's own. In the example just given, the process is made simpler because both husband and wife know the broad framework within which they are working – husband as breadwinner, wife as homemaker – and they agree upon it. Often it is not so simple. Problems arise when people become uncomfortable with the guidelines they use to organize and make sense of their lives.

One way in which this can happen is when people are faced with situations to which their guidelines do not apply. Consider, for example, a woman who believes that a woman's role is first and foremost that of wife and mother, and whose husband thinks that housework and childcare are 'women's jobs'. What happens if she has to go out to work because the family needs money? She is doing two jobs – both of which put heavy demands on her time and energy. In sociologists' terms, she experiences 'role strain'. This is defined by Goode (1960) as 'the felt difficulty in fulfilling role obligations' (Goode 1960:483). She is under pressure because she is trying to take on a new role, while keeping her old ones intact.

A different kind of problem arises when people no longer agree about the basic role divisions. Komarovsky (1946) thought that changes in women's roles in this century had placed many contradictory and inconsistent demands upon women. Women college students, when asked to write about themselves, complained that their families had conflicting expectations of them. They were told, on the one hand to do well academically, and on the other, to act 'feminine' and play down their abilities, in order to get a husband. They could not possibly satisfy both sets of expectations at once. One woman commented: 'It seemed that my family had expected me to become Eve Curie and Hedy Lamar wrapped up in one.'

It is not only conflicting demands from others that are a problem. People can also have conflicting views of themselves. They do not know what they 'want' or 'ought' to do.

Role conflict is defined by Thomas and Biddle (1966) as:

(1) 'Inconsistent prescriptions (or other standards) held for a person by himself or by one or more others.'
(2) 'The attributions of inconsistent prescriptions or standards to others, applicable to one's self.'
(3) 'Feelings of unease resulting from the existence or assumption of inconsistent prescriptions (or standards).'

(Thomas and Biddle 1966 : 12)

This definition outlines some of the problems. But it does make it sound again, like choosing shoes. It gives the impression that the alternatives are there, so that all people have to do is to choose between them and get others to agree.

It seems to us that this is not always so. Very often, when people are unhappy with their roles, the alternatives are not there ready-made. They have to be invented. And it can be quite difficult to know how to go about it. One problem is that new guidelines have to be developed. Another is that the various roles that a woman has, are interconnected – so that a change in one area has repercussions on the rest of life. Yet another problem is to get other people to play their part – and these other people may include not only a husband, but also children, relatives, family friends, the boss at work, and the Government – when the others have a vested interest in *not* changing.

Let us look at some of the effects that taking on a work role can have on a woman's image of herself as a wife and mother. And conversely, at the influence that being a wife and mother has on her image of herself at work.

Several studies have shown that mothers expect paid work to lead to problems in running the home and looking after the children. They feel anxious and guilty about their possible inadequacy as mothers (see Nye 1974b for review). Many give this as their reason for not working.

When the woman is deeply involved in her career, the strain is even greater. Fogarty, Rapoport, and Rapoport (1971) made an intensive study of 'dual-career families'. These were families in which both husband and wife were committed to a demanding professional career as well as having children. All the couples felt that they faced very great practical and psychological demands. They thought that good physical health and immense energy were essential to make the 'dual-career family' possible. One husband said: 'We're never ill in any serious sense, and I think that we attach more importance to that one fact for our survival capacity than anything else.'

This is an interesting remark, because it suggests that the husband is under strain too. Presumably he has taken on some of the responsibility for running the home. There has been a good deal of research on the effects of a wife's paid employment on the division of labour within the home, and on the wife's power. Bahr (1974) concludes from a review that, 'In general the wife's power tends to increase when she becomes employed, although power is contingent on other factors, and more powerful wives are more likely to become employed' (Bahr 1974 : 184–5). In particular, the working wife has more power in decisions concerning finance, and rather less within the household. Lower-class wives may gain more power by working than middle-class wives, perhaps because the contribution they make by working is seen as greater.

In general, most studies of the division of labour in the home suggests that husbands of working wives tend to take more share in housework. As we have seen in Chapter 2, many employed wives want their husbands to do more housework. But the wife who wants, or actually persuades, her husband to take equal shares, is extremely unusual.

How do these changes and adjustments affect the relationship between husband and wife?

Nye (1974a) concludes that early studies showed slightly more marital problems among employed wives. However, more recent studies show no difference for middle-class women, but some differences favouring the non-employed for working-class women. This one would expect, considering that working-class women face more practical difficulties in combining the two roles, and are also less likely to have husbands who can make adjustments in their work.

Marriage and motherhood also affect work. Many of the effects are obvious, and have already been outlined. Because of their family roles, women are more likely not to work. They tend to be less committed to their work than men. They seldom get high status or highly-paid jobs. Single women graduates, as compared with married women, more often say that their greatest satisfaction comes from work. Also, the career aspirations of single graduates rise after leaving university, whereas the career aspirations of married graduates fall (Fogarty, Rapoport, and Rapoport 1971).

However, motherhood can in certain circumstances have a rather different effect on work. Haller and Rosenmayr (1971), in the study mentioned earlier, found that, among middle-class Austrian women, those with children were more committed to their jobs than women who did not yet have children. Other researchers have found the same (Sobol 1963; Fogarty, Rapoport, and Rapoport 1971). Bailyn (1964) suggests that women have an over-idealized picture of motherhood. They expect that when they have children they will want to devote their time to them, to the exclusion of everything else. Actual experience of children dampens their idealism and work becomes more attractive as a result – but only for middle-class women (Haller and Rosenmayr 1971).

Farmer and Bohn (1970) wondered how women would feel about their careers if they faced less prejudice and fewer practical difficulties in combining career and family. Fifty women from a Business and Professional Women's Club were asked to fill in a questionnaire measuring their commitment to their careers. They were then asked to fill in the questionnaire once again pretending that: (1) men like intelligent women; (2) men and women are equally promoted in business and the professions; and (3) raising a family well is very possible for a career woman. As Farmer and Bohn predicted, the women's career commitment scores rose second time round.

Gordon and Hall (1974) thought that the role conflicts a woman experiences would be influenced by: (1) her image of herself; (2) her view of femininity; and (3) what she thinks men think. They asked 229 college-educated women to complete a questionnaire. They used three semantic differentials. First, the women rated themselves on twenty-eight bi-polar 7-point adjective scales. Second, they rated their concepts of a 'feminine woman' on the same scales. Finally, using the same scales again, they described what they thought the 'average man' would think a 'feminine woman' is like.

In order to find out how the twenty-eight qualities were seen as related to each other, Gordon and Hall performed a factor analysis on each of the three sets of ratings. This showed that the women were using four main dimensions (or factors) when they made their judgments. The first dimension, which they called 'potency', was made up of descriptions of emotional and physical strength. The second dimension, which they called 'supportiveness', comprised looking after people and being generally pleasant socially. The third, termed 'spontaneity', referred to a person's willingness to take immediate action; while the fourth, termed 'emotionality', described strength of feelings of various kinds.

Another part of the research asked the women: '(a) What conflicts or strains, if any, have you experienced between your various roles in life? (b) How do you deal with these conflicts? (c) Overall, how satisfied do you feel with the way you deal with your roles in life? (d) In general, how happy would you say you are?'

One quarter of the women reported no conflicts. The most common conflict, acknowledged by about one third of the women, was between their roles at home and their roles outside the home (i.e. mainly at work).

Did attitudes to femininity make any difference to the amount of conflict experienced? It turned out that neither a woman's view of herself nor her idea of what a 'feminine' woman was like, was related to whether or not she experienced conflict.

However, her image of a man's image of a feminine woman did make a significant difference. All four of the dimensions which emerged from the analysis of the rating scales were significantly related to the conflict between home and non-home roles. Thus, the less potent and the more emotional a woman

127

thought men think women are, the more conflicts of this kind she had. Moreover, women who thought that a man's image of a feminine woman would be different from the way they saw themselves, also had more conflicts about roles.

Unfortunately, we are not given information about the men in these women's lives. It could be that their conflicts arose from a mistaken idea of what men want in a woman. Or it could be that they had conflicts because the men they had to deal with really did see women this way.

The discrepancy between a woman's image of herself and her image of a feminine woman was important in a different way. In particular, the less 'supportive' a woman felt, by comparison with her image of a feminine woman, the more likely she was to experience conflict between different roles within the home.

Perhaps surprisingly, when we turn to the question of satisfaction and happiness, a rather different picture emerges. Neither a woman's concept of a feminine woman, nor her concept of a man's views, made any difference to satisfaction and happiness. It was her image of herself which was important. The more potent, supportive, and unemotional a woman felt herself to be, the more satisfied and happy she was. Gordon and Hall comment that 'Whatever male influence exists appears to have its limits. Ultimately, it seems to be the woman's own self-image that determines her overall satisfaction and happiness' (Gordon and Hall 1974:243). It is interesting that the particular qualities which are linked with happiness seem to include some which are found in other studies to be stereotypically seen as 'masculine' (potent, unemotional), and some which are seen as 'feminine' (supportive).

Changing roles and making new ones – strategies for dealing with pressure, strain, and conflict

How do women deal with the pressures and conflicting demands that their roles place upon them? And how do they resolve the conflicts within themselves?

One way, of course, is avoidance. Some women simply do not take on roles which would interfere with the roles most important to them. Rossi (1965a) found that single women graduates in jobs which are unusual for women, described themselves as 'occupationally competitive' more often than married women in similar jobs. Perhaps they stayed single because they foresaw that marriage would hamper their ambitions. Conversely, mothers may choose not to work.

For women who want to be wives *and* mothers *and* workers, the problems are rather different. In the study by Fogarty, Rapoport, and Rapoport (1971), on dual-career families, several of the women described themselves as being very different people at home and at work. One woman put it like this: 'When I'm at work I'm very authoritarian. I wear a white coat at work and I try to hang up my working personality with it when I leave the office.' (Her husband confirmed this; when he saw her at work, 'She seemed like someone else – some sort of tycoon – certainly not my wife.') Another woman said: 'I am two different people at home and at work ... I am much more domineering and aggressive in the office than I am at home in that I will fight a point in the office in a way that I would never fight in a domestic situation, or want to.' These women seem to feel that the qualities they need at work would cause problems in the family. They deal with the discrepancy by making a sharp distinction between the two.

Poloma (1972) thinks that most women cope, to their own satisfaction, with the pressures from their different roles. They do not feel under serious strain, or in conflict. She interviewed fifty-three married couples in which the wife was actively engaged in the practice of law, medicine, or college teaching. (She chose these professions because they require a 'male-type' commitment to work – in her view.) Husband and wife were interviewed separately using an interview schedule developed by Rapoport and Rapoport (Fogarty, Rapoport, and Rapoport 1971). She found that the amount of practical conflict varied with the stage of the woman's working career. Training was the worst phase because it was impossible to limit the demands of work to fit in with the family. Conflict also varied with the age of the children. She concluded that her women were basically satisfied; only eight of the fifty-three cases showed what she considered to be 'persistent unresolved role strain'. Most of the women gave the roles of wife and mother precedence over their professional lives. They dealt with conflicting demands on their time by taking part-time work or quitting work when the children were small. At this stage they treated their jobs as 'work' rather than 'career'.

Poloma describes a number of techniques by which the women managed the tensions involved:

(1) 'favourable definition of the situation'; for example, saying to yourself 'I am a better mother because I work'.
(2) deciding which is the most important role to them; for example, (usually) putting family demands first.
(3) 'Compartmentalization' – keeping roles separate in their minds and in practice. (She notes that few women brought their work home, though husbands often did.)
(4) 'Compromise'; for example, cutting down their career involvement to fit in with the various demands.

One interesting point here is that both Poloma and her interviewees seem to have assumed that the dilemma had to be resolved by the wife. No mention is made of the possibility of changing role relationships with the husband. No one asked the husband to 'compromise' about his career. No one suggested that he put family demands first.

Hall (1972) came to a different conclusion. In his study, the married women workers were under more pressure, and had more conflicts about their roles when they had young children. They were also less satisfied with the way they managed their roles. He suggests that different women use different strategies for managing conflict. One strategy is to change the demands that are placed on the woman by others. This involves changing the attitudes and behaviour of other people – that is changing the role, in fact. He called this 'structural role definition'. Another strategy is to change the demands that the woman makes of herself and the way she sees herself. He called this 'personal role definition'. A quite different approach is to try to meet *all* the expectations that other people have of her in *all* her different roles. Women who did this were assuming that roles cannot or must not be changed. *They* must satisfy everyone. In the attempt to do this, some women planned their lives elaborately. They organized themselves. They worked harder and harder. Hall called this 'reactive role behaviour'. He thought that it was not really a strategy for coping at all. What he seems to mean by this is that they are not really facing the fact that the demands made on them are unreasonably high – and perhaps impossible to fulfil. Because of this, they are not choosing a strategy that could actually cope with the problem.

Hall also carried out a study of the coping strategies used by college-educated women. He found, of course, that many women used a mixture of strategies. But the women who made more use of 'structural role definition' were generally more satisfied, whereas women who resorted mainly to 'reactive role behaviour' tended to be less so.

Another study (Gordon and Hall 1974) showed that the kind of strategy a woman used was related to the way she saw herself. In particular, women who saw themselves as more 'supportive' (that is more 'nurturant' and more 'agreeable in inter-personal settings') tended to cope by structurally redefining their roles, and not by trying to meet all demands. Women who saw themselves as more 'supportive', 'potent', and 'un-emotional' were also more satisfied with the way they managed their roles. And they were happier.

It looks as if, for married women, the route to satisfaction and happiness lies in changing their roles somewhat. But whether or not a woman sees her way to doing this depends in part on the way she sees herself.

This is hardly surprising. Making new roles is a difficult busi-ness. It involves changing other people's roles as well as one's own. And the more dramatic the change, the more difficult it is – and the more hostile the reactions of even well-intentioned others.

Some of the problems are illustrated in one woman's account of her attempts to get her husband to take equal shares in housework. They had no children. Both of them were working. She decided that it was unfair that the housework should be left to her. At the same time she loved her husband and wanted to stay married. She was lucky, in that he also believed in equality, and also wanted to stay married to her. Nonethe-less: 'It is up to us to remember that men are conditioned to expect servicing, and even if they acknowledge equality in theory, they will relax all too soon into the role society prepares them for.' She had to reappraise her own standards: 'Was it really necessary to keep dusting and cleaning? ... Together we had to work out a common definition of "dirty" and "untidy".' Finally, they agreed to take turns on the major chores. But that was not the end of the story:

'He absolutely refused (and still does) to clean the loo ...'

'When it came to washing, Dave worked to rule. He never realised the need of tackling the dirty socks under the bed, or the occasional washing like curtains and dressing gowns ... Similarly, he pretended not to understand the process of sorting out colours. After a few of my pale things had been ruined, I had to start teaching him. *He* never minded if his handkerchiefs were the colour of his Levis.'

'All this pretence at ignorance, I found, is an exercise in defiance. Men can't really be that stupid. He not only succeeded in making me feel like a tyrant, but also failed to lighten my load, as I had to think about his turn as well as mine.'   (Whitfield 1976:6–7)

Stephenson (1973b) studied the process by which some women come to make changes in their roles. She was interested in the women's own views of the way they decide what they want and set about getting it. After nearly a year of participant observation of two women's liberation groups, she interviewed group members who had been involved in the group for at least six months.

She found that there were four themes which were always present in their accounts. First, they had become aware of the expectations that society had of 'housewives'. Second, they were unhappy about having to meet all these expectations. Third, they began to reinterpret their situation. Usually, this happened when they heard about some part of the Women's Liberation Movement ideology which they could apply to themselves. But fourth, in order to work out how to change, and to carry it through, they had all needed the support of the woman's group. The first three themes appear in the following account:

'... I felt awfully trapped and not able to do things

because ... I had two kids and my husband was really quite unco-operative about looking after them at that point ...'

'I felt I was giving up my entire existence – which I was – and my entire self to him and our kids ... I always felt if I was taking any time for myself I was just being selfish and, after all, a good married woman was to devote herself to her family ...'

'That's why I found The Feminine Mystique, which talks quite a bit about housewifery and boredom and isolation and loneliness – which I was experiencing – quite meaningful to me. More than field of employment or ... media things ... It didn't mean as much to me as it did to find out there were other women who were ... as confused as I was. I was mostly just confused. I didn't know what I should be doing.'   (Stephenson 1973b:250–1)

Most of the women came to a woman's group through a friend who was already involved. At this point they were mostly still fairly unsure about what they wanted. Through talking with other women, each woman began to define the specific areas that she personally wanted to change – in herself as well as others. With the support of the group, she could start to experiment outside.

One woman, for instance, wanted to involve her husband more in housework. This is her view of how she set about it:

'We rarely fight ... usually we try to talk them (disagreements) out. Sometimes its a matter of having a few conversations about it over a period of time, maybe a couple of weeks, maybe a couple of days. It just depends ... There are separate actions going on so you have a conversation and you do something a little differently and you sort of see how it lays. And then, you know, you have another little conversation and do something else which either compensates for something that was wrong with the first action or goes one step ahead.'   (Stephenson 1973b:253)

More far-reaching changes

All the evidence we have looked at in this chapter has been from Western countries, and usually in the setting of a nuclear family. These are societies which basically accept a particular view of sex roles. Thus, two important limitations have to be borne in mind. Firstly, if we looked at women in other countries, we should expect to find that they have different views on sex roles, and rather different problems and conflicts (see Rosaldo and Lamphere 1974).

The second limitation concerns the studies of the way in which women set about reorganizing and changing their roles. The social and economic context puts limits on what any individual woman can do. On her own, she can sometimes opt out of expected roles, by staying single, staying childless, etc. Or, she can negotiate with her partner to reorganize roles within the family; so that the woman does paid work, or the man takes part in housework and childcare, for instance. What she cannot do, alone, is to make role changes that depend upon people outside the family. She cannot force an employer to let her work hours which fit in with childcare, without penalizing her through low wages and a dead-end job. She cannot make the State provide nurseries so that she can work when the children are small. She cannot compel her partner's employer to give him shorter hours so that he can do some housework. Thus, it is hardly surprising that the women whose attempts at role changes we described talk mainly about their own particular families. They assume that this is where changes can be made.

There have been many experimental attempts by whole communities to change the sex roles of all their members, in various ways, and with different degrees of success. Today, many communes are trying to change the relationship between work and family life, and the way children are brought up (see, for example, Berger, Hackett, and Millar 1972; Gordon 1972). Over the past 200 years, in England and America, there have been numerous 'Utopian' communities, with heterogeneous ideologies, which attempted, among other things, to weaken the ties between man and wife, in order to strengthen their allegiance to the community as a whole (Muncy 1974; Gollin 1972). In Israel, the early kibbutzim organized washing, cooking, and childcare communally (Schlesinger 1972) though this work is still more often done by women (Tiger and Shepher 1975; Bernard 1976).

134

In Russia, after the revolution, state kitchens and comprehensive state nurseries were set up, the latter being still in existence (Rowbotham 1972, Chapter 6; Bronfenbrenner 1970). Myrdal (1965) reports an interesting account, by one Chinese woman, of the way village women worked together to change their roles and their beliefs during the course of the Chinese revolution.

We need to know more about what the women in these different situations felt about the large-scale changes, whether made by them or imposed upon them. What conflicts and problems did they face? What strategies did they use to cope with them?

EIGHT

Sex

The shortness of this chapter speaks for itself. There is hardly any information about what women think of sexual intercourse or about sex generally. Those who deviate from society's sexual code have been studied a great deal but, again, as objects and not as subjects. Is part of the reason the fact that, because woman has been a sex object in society for so long, few have thought it interesting to ask her what she thinks about sex herself? What we can be clear on is that society's view on what is sexually appropriate will have a profound effect on what goes on in bed. And so, apparently, does social class.

Rainwater (1968) has pointed out that sexual pleasure is related to social class in that the more reported satisfaction there is, the higher is likely to be the class. This, in turn, may be connected to sexual experience comparisons between races. Liben (1969) for instance, concluded from a study of fifty-three unmarried pregnant black women that the women rarely reported any sexual pleasure from sexual intercourse. This is quite contrary to the stereotype of the Negro, whose sexual act is supposed to be 'uninhibited, spontaneous, and highly pleasurable'. Since Liben's women were virtually all working-class, this finding of little sexual pleasure is consistent with the earlier results. The environment is more likely to determine attitudes and behaviour than are genes.

A different type of study has been concerned with investigating the sexual behaviour of college students. In one such study, D'Augelli and Cross (1975) interviewed 119 unmarried college women to find out their attitudes to premarital sex, parents' attitudes, and so forth. They related these to the women's actual stated sexual behaviour based on responses to the Sex Experience Inventory (Brady and Levitt 1965).

From the interview data, the women were classified as: (a) inexperienced virgins; (b) adamant virgins; (c) potential non-virgins; (d) engaged non-virgins; (e) liberated non-virgins; and (f) confused non-virgins. On the basis of the Sex Experience Inventory, the women were classified into five categories:

'(a) *neckers* – those who have engaged in kissing and/or tongue kissing; (b) *light petters* – those who have engaged in any of the above plus manual manipulation of and/or oral contact with clad or unclad breasts; (c) *heavy petters* – those who have engaged in any of the above plus manual manipulation of the genitalia of or by the partner; (d) *technical virgins* – those who have engaged in any of the above plus oral–genital contact of or by the partner; and (e) *non-virgins* – those who have engaged in any of the above plus intercourse, front–front or front–back.' (D'Augelli and Cross 1975:42)

Their results showed that sex guilt was negatively related to sexual experience. That is, the more liberal was the woman's philosophy the less guilt she experienced and the more actual premarital sexual experience she had. These authors cite Ehrmann (1959) as having found that women experienced less guilt about sexual activity when they felt the relationship was an important one.

Apart from experiencing guilt about premarital sexual behaviour, women also feel guilt to varying degrees about fantasizing during sexual intercourse. For instance, there has been some controversy about whether women or men have more fantasies. De Martino (1969) studied 102 women. They were interviewed and 44 per cent reported having fantasies of some sort. These varied from thoughts of another man to group orgies, sub-jugation and homosexuality. But as these women were nudists, it is possible that they were not wholly representative of the general population of the United States!

There are several existing theories about fantasies, most stemming from Freud's statement that, 'A happy person never phantasizes, only an unsatisfied one' (Freud 1962:146). Clinicians will therefore view a confession to having fantasies during intercourse as an indication of a 'neurotic character'. But Singer (1966), for example, is of the opinion that fantasies may reflect the cognitive skill of the individual. Some women are practised day-dreamers who indulge in it during many situa-tions, of which sexual intercourse is one. The guilt and anxiety felt by women in this context and reported by clinicians may not be a reflection of the 'neurotic feminine character' but due to a feeling that such fantasies are abnormal and contrary to the cultural stereotype of the female. Contrary to the psycho-analytic model, Singer's model of fantasy leads one to see it as a means of enhancing sexual arousal. It is an adaptive response to the passive sex-role, slow sexual build-up, or an escape from the unpleasant reality of dissatisfaction with the husband.

So Hariton and Singer (1974) studied the fantasies of 141 upper-middle-class married women in a New York suburb. They had been married for an average of ten years. As with so many studies, care must be taken before generalizations from these results can be made to other female populations, since 75 per cent of the women were Jewish and 20 per cent Catholic. They were asked to complete a day-dreaming inventory. Part One contained five scales to do with fear of failure, guilt, positive reactions, future-orientation, and acceptance of day-dreaming. Part Two consisted of 'stimulus-dependent' positive thoughts, which were direct reactions to the husband and involved warmth, tenderness, or excitement; while negative thoughts in-cluded feelings of revulsion or dissatisfaction with what the hus-band was doing at that moment, distracting thoughts that in-volved such things as listening to noises in the house, thinking about the day's activities, and awareness of irrelevant stimuli. Part Three consisted of scales to measure the 'stimulus-independent' thoughts which were in the form of fifteen erotic fantasy items. Examples included 'I imagine that I am being overpowered or forced to surrender'; 'Thoughts of an imaginary romantic lover enter my mind'; 'I pretend that I'm a whore or prostitute'. There were other pencil and paper tests and fifty-six of the women were interviewed as well. These interviews were used as a check on the general accuracy of the inventory responses about erotic fantasies and also to develop a clinical, composite picture of each person.

Hariton and Singer believe that theirs is the first report of fantasies during sexual intercourse described by a fair-sized sample of married women. The results can lead one to conclude that fantasizing during intercourse is normal, at least among upper-middle-class married American Jewish women, since 65 per cent reported having erotic fantasies some time during intercourse, and 37 per cent reported having fantasies very often. If this is so for the population of women in general, then fantasizing can no longer be said to be the product of the neurotic female mind.

The frequency of occurrence of the different types of fantasy is of some interest as can be seen in *Table 6* below.

What can it mean that 56 per cent of these women had fantasies during sexual intercourse of an imaginary romantic lover? Is this just general dissatisfaction with the partner? Or can it be, as Singer suggests, that this type of fantasy enhances the erotic experience? The fact that the fantasy of being over-powered comes near the top of the list is not too surprising if it is presumed (for it is not stated) that the most common sexual position is for the man to be lying on top of the woman rather than *vice versa*. It would be interesting to know whether men and women's fantasies differ according to the position in which intercourse takes place. Do men have fantasies of being raped if in the submissive position?

In her book, *My Secret Garden* (1975), Friday gives an account of the sexual fantasies sent in to her by women in response to advertisements she placed in magazines. Her aim was not to analyse them but to help women understand that, indeed, it is a desirable thing to have fantasies, and to help remove the guilt many women feel, as well as the belief that they are in some way abnormal for having sometimes quite bizarre thoughts – bizarre, that is, in the cold light of day.

Table 6 Frequency of occurrence of each of the fifteen fantasies described in the erotic fantasy scale.

item	incidence
thoughts of an imaginary romantic lover enter my mind	56·0
I relive a previous sexual experience	52·0
I enjoy pretending that I am doing something wicked or forbidden	49·6
I imagine that I am being overpowered or forced to surrender	48·9
I am in a different place like a car, motel, beach, woods, etc.	46·8
I imagine myself delighting many men	43·2
I pretend that I struggle and resist before being aroused to surrender	39·7
I imagine that I am observing myself or others having sex	38·3
I pretend that I am another irresistibly sexy female	37·6
I daydream that I am being made love to by more than one man at a time	35·5
my thoughts center about feelings of weakness or helplessness	33·3
I see myself as a striptease dancer, harem girl, or other performer	28·4
I pretend that I am a whore or a prostitute	24·9
I imagine that I am forced to expose my body to a seducer	19·1
my fantasies center around urination or defecation	2·1

(Source: Hariton and Singer 1974:317)

So there is good evidence that fantasies during sexual intercourse are normal. The other area that has been looked at is the degree to which women respond to erotic literature. In one such study, Izard and Caplan (1974) gave male and female college students either an erotic passage or part of an academic text to read. Their feelings were then measured by their completing an 'emotions' scale both before and after reading.

The results showed that, whereas there had been no sex difference on the scale before reading, after reading the erotic passage men reported more sexual arousal, interest, and joy, and women reported more disgust. However, the authors point out that the sex differences in interest, joy, and disgust were less than the differences between those females reading the academic, and those reading the erotic passage. That is, the change was greater between the female groups than between the male and female groups.

But filling out questionnaires about one's state of sexual arousal is a somewhat indirect measure of feelings. And Heiman's work (1975) suggests that it is liable to produce misleading results for women. It is obvious that, whereas men have a clear and visible indication of sexual arousal, the same is not true for women. Heiman found that about 50 per cent of the women studied who were highly aroused by erotic tape-recordings reported that they felt no physical response.

To enable her to make such statements, she had a group of seventy-seven college students fit a small acrylic cylinder containing a photocell and light source into the vagina. This photocell registers diffused light as vaginal pressure pulse and blood volume change. Both these responses have been shown by Masters and Johnson (1966) to relate to sexual arousal. Female and male students were divided into three groups and listened to either four erotic stories, four romantic tapes (no explicit sex), or romantic–erotic tapes (couples expressed affection and had sex), or else they listened to tapes of couples sharing conversation, dinner, or wine 'but not each other'.

It was the sex and not the romance that was the stimulator both for men and for women. In fact, the women rated the erotic tapes as more arousing than did the men. One of the stories was found to be particularly arousing to the women. In this story a woman was the central figure and also the initiator of the sex behaviour. But Heiman says she was fascinated in the finding that both men and women preferred the female as initiator. She puts forward several explanations for this finding, including the one that the female students liked the idea of control and the men the opportunity 'to lie back and enjoy it, without having to worry about performance' (Heiman 1975:60).

A finding which supports the work on sexual fantasy is that the women as well as the men were able to become sexually aroused by simply being told to fantasize.

As well as having physiological measures of arousal, Heiman asked the students whether or not they felt aroused. There was a high correlation between the two measures both for men and women, but the women made more mistakes than the men. Heiman found that the women who made the most mistakes about their state of sexual arousal were the ones who were listening to the non-erotic tapes. She says it was as if these women were denying or ignoring their physiological changes in the absence of a good reason as to why they should feel sexy.

That there is still an inordinate amount to be learned about women's attitudes to their own bodies, can be seen by the very fact that it was thought necessary to have a long and prolonged debate about whether there is one or two types of female orgasm.

Comments

We could write another book here or else let the facts (or lack of them) speak for themselves. Clearly, the sexual behaviour men and women indulge in is, to a very large extent, determined by sex-role stereotypes. The sexual act itself is perhaps the ultimate in the dominance–submission relationship but it also allows women to show some aggression. The more aggressive the man is the more the woman can show aggression since she will still not be perceived as dominating the relationship.

NINE

Pregnancy and childbirth

The desire to be a mother

Whatever the developmental process may be, there are many
women whose core concern is to be a mother. This will imply
different things to different women, but the common ground is
the overriding desire to have a baby. For these women there can
doubtless be few more rewarding experiences. But this is not
necessarily the case for all women. There are many for whom
motherhood may be a pleasant and even desirable state but for
whom, as has been shown in Chapter 5, the acceptance of this
role will cause conflict with other core-role constructs, such as
making a success of a career. For these latter women, we may
expect adjustment to pregnancy to be difficult.

The desire for motherhood starts young. Middle-class American girls between the ages of five and eleven increasingly dislike the thought of work outside the home as they get older,
seeming to prefer the cultural stereotype of home, husband, and
children (Hartley 1960). Hartley also found no reason to believe

that these attitudes were changing with the years, as an increasing number of middle-class women began following careers.

In their report on the changes in attitudes of British children as they increase in age from seven to fifteen, Moore and Clautour (1977) point out that a significant proportion of both boys and girls say they want to get married, but that the girls desiring marriage far outnumber the boys (by as much as 32 per cent at ages twelve and fifteen). The other side of the coin is also of interest. The 'no' vote at age seven was 17 per cent for boys and only 8 per cent for girls, and at age twelve, the gap was even wider – 23 per cent to 4 per cent respectively. However, by age fifteen, the boys also seem to have got the message and only 9 per cent voted against marriage compared with 2 per cent for girls.

The picture is much the same with regard to desiring children. The majority of both boys and girls want children, but substantially more of the girls do so at all ages. Reasons given for wanting to get married and have children varied according to age. Apart from children being a general reason for getting married, seven-year-olds liked the idea of the wedding, honeymoon, and all the clothes and household paraphernalia that go with it. As they got older, companionship and love were given as common reasons by both sexes. It should be noted that at twelve, more boys than girls hoped to be looked after by their partner!

Both social class and intelligence made a difference to attitudes. It was the girls of higher social class and intelligence who most wanted to be married and also to have children. This would suggest that higher class and intelligence lead to better 'learning' of sex-role stereotypes, but as they are also those who are more likely to want to go on to further education and perhaps a career, they are building up some considerable conflict for themselves.

Moore and Clautour point out that very similar findings have come from studies of other populations of children. For instance, with a sample of Stockholm children (Klackenberg-Larsson 1974); Norwegian children (Nordland 1973); French children (Zazzo 1956); and Danish children (Diderichsen *et al.* 1975).

144

All agree that such attitudes are the result of early education and social norms. Differing attitudes resulting from different cultures have been studied by Bronfenbrenner (1970), who looked at childrearing in the Soviet Union, and by Kessen (1975) who reported recently on childrearing in the People's Republic of China.

But as far as our own culture is concerned, we may be proud of how well we instil the sex stereotype into young children. Their hopes about children and marriage are also likely to be realized. For about 80 per cent of adults in England and Wales do become parents, and the figures are not very different for other Western countries. It is therefore not surprising that it is held up as an ideal state – one should want children since this is the social norm. Moreover, the children reflect the social norm of seeing parenthood as being intimately tied in with marriage. It is expected and considered desirable for those who marry to want to have children and, conversely, it is expected that those who want to have children will marry. It is not a question of 'are you going to have children?' but 'when are you going to have children?'

MacIntyre (1976) spells out the problems relating to research into the psychological understanding of reproduction. Sex, marriage, and reproduction are bracketed together so that there is the disincentive to carry out research on one of these aspects alone.

'Though sex, marriage and reproduction may be linked empirically in a particular society and its dominant ideology, we still need to enquire into the processes leading to them and the meanings attributed to them. We cannot assume *a priori* that people have babies because they are married, or marry in order to have babies; nor that people have babies because they have had sex, or that they have sex in order to produce babies.' (MacIntyre 1976 : 152)

In fact, birth and marriage are not as inevitably intertwined as society would like. Busfield (1974) gives the Registrar General's figures for 1966–7 indicating that illegitimate births in Britain were only eighty-four per 1,000. But of legitimate births to women who had no previous children, about 25 per cent

145

were conceived before marriage, rising to 40 per cent for those under twenty years old. In the US it is estimated that up to 25 per cent of pregnancies are unwanted by one or both parents (Bumpass and Westoff 1970). This relationship between conception and marriage is a good indication of the strength of the social stigma attached to illegitimacy at the present time. But premarital conception is fast becoming the norm for the young – at least it was in 1966 and 1967 in Britain.

These strong social pressures on women to marry and have children continue, despite the fact that only about one quarter of their lives will be spent childbearing and looking after the children when young. The negative image of the woman who does not have children plays an important part here. The childless woman is not a proper female. Similarly, her real role in society is to be a mother and a wife. The opposite role to being a wife is to be a spinster which also has negative implications. But the same is not necessarily so for men, whose roles of father and husband are not usually their sole roles, nor their most important. To be a bachelor is socially acceptable and even has several very positive connotations.

But the soft sell by society of the mother role has a success rate that must be the envy of many a salesman. Busfield (1974) tells how she and some colleagues interviewed 290 couples in 1969 and 1970 asking them 'how different do you think your lives would be without children?'. They replied in terms of loneliness, emptiness, and boredom. Kelly (1955) talks of the construing of oneself in some very personally significant way, as core-role construing. For some, the fundamentally important idea of being 'a wife' or 'a mother' or 'a career woman' is what 'maintains' them. We are all seen as having some such core-role constructs, although only a limited number. But if we have only one – such as being 'a mother' – then there really *is* nothing but boredom and emptiness, without *proof* that one is fulfilling that role. So marriage and pregnancy become the evidence needed to validate our view of our purpose in life. But is this validating evidence really satisfying? And, if so, to whom?

Hubert (1974) talked to a sample of married working-class women who were expecting their first babies. She used no questionnaires or structure for the interviews, she simply talked to each woman. She looked first at conception, both the facts and the women's views on the process. Two-thirds of the pregnancies were not planned and about a half of these were unwelcome. These 'mistakes' were all the result of the couple using ineffective birth control methods – withdrawal being the most widely practised. She found that there was a surprising lack of knowledge about the process of conception. One woman thought that if she took Beechams Pills after intercourse it would 'clear you all through'. Another thought all would be well if one sat on the lavatory afterwards so that it 'would all come out'.

Gross inadequacy of knowledge about conception and contraception was also found by Liben (1969). She studied fifty-three pregnant unmarried black women, with ages ranging from thirteen to thirty-six years. Ignorance of the nature of conception was, not surprisingly, commonest among the young. But it was apparently not confined to that group, since one twenty-nine-year-old is cited as having stated that she thought she would not become pregnant if she got no pleasure from the intercourse. Liben says that it is not an uncommon belief in that group of people, 'Ignorance of sexual anatomy, physiology, and functioning was abysmal' (Liben 1969 : 1874). It is unfortunate for these women that the myth is not true, since they rarely reported experiencing any pleasure from intercourse or orgasm. If the myth were true at least they would not have to use any form of contraception or have unwanted babies. The two girls in the study who reported experiencing pleasurable orgasms, both married the 'father'. Attitudes to marriage among these women were mixed. Some were more successful in their jobs than their male partners and more 'upwardly mobile'. So marriage for them would be regarded by the man as a threat, since he would risk the exposure of his inadequacy to support a wife and child. Also, with public assistance, the women were definitely better off unmarried. Few had considered abortion, but they were poor and abortions can be expensive in the United States. Similarly, few wanted to offer their babies for adoption, but perhaps this was also realistic in a culture where it is very difficult to find adoptive homes for black babies.

In general, Liben says that the women did not take their pregnancy lightly, many were ashamed and felt guilt. They had 'bought' the American dream, 'a house in the suburbs, marriage, and an ideal family of two or three children (occasionally four). Their ambitions for the children were for them to have what they themselves had lacked; a middle-class education, occupation and income' (Liben 1969 : 1876).

Whether marriage is an important factor in determining the desire for a baby or not, there are one quarter of a million unplanned pregnancies in Britain each year. 'Of these only half are accepted. Of those not accepted, half end in abortion, spontaneous or induced, and the remainder go on to term in family situations likely to produce anti-social adjustment' (Jacobs 1972 : 17). Some 500 pregnant women come to a weekly session at the Marie Stopes Memorial Centre, and 80 per cent of these are between seventeen and twenty-five years old, unmarried, and belonging to skilled or semi-skilled groups. Almost all know about conception, contraception, and where to obtain advice, and yet 40 per cent used no contraception and a further 40 per cent used it very irregularly. But perhaps here 'knowing' is one thing and 'believing' another.

Jacobs comments that the 1967 *Abortion Law* in England enables a woman and her doctor to request termination of her unwanted pregnancy, if the medico-social circumstances are unfavourable. 'The steady flow of requests for abortion shows that the climate of public opinion has changed to incorporate Sir Dugald Baird's Fifth Freedom – "freedom from the tyranny of excess fertility" – and to establish the birthright of every child – "that he be wanted" ' (Jacobs 1972 : 17). But things are not always as easy as this in practice, even if the law is not soon changed.

This lack of wholehearted enthusiasm for having bonny bouncing babies as the female stereotype dictates, is not just a product of the permissive society. For in 1933, Hall and Mohr interviewed sixty-six expectant mothers who were pregnant for

148

the first time. None had private physicians and all were mainly first generation Americans ranging in age from sixteen to thirty-six years. Forty-eight were Catholic, sixteen Protestant, and two Jewish. Seventy-seven per cent used no contraception and 65 per cent had not planned the pregnancy. However, it must be borne in mind that forty-eight were Catholics. But whether planned or not, only eleven fully accepted the pregnancy, another forty-one were still not reconciled. Ten had tried to terminate the pregnancy.

The most common reason given by these women for rejecting the pregnancy was lack of money, then came just a desire to postpone parenthood, then fear of danger to the child because of poor heredity. There were several superstitious beliefs about characteristics thought to be transmitted genetically – for example: 'Will my baby grow up to be bad ... My husband is a thief and a gangster. Brags about the many girls he has ruined. I wish the baby would die. What can you expect from a father like that?' (Hall and Mohr 1933:229). Several other reasons were given for not wanting to be pregnant at that time, but only two women gave their actual dislike of children as their reason.

A few years later, Thompson (1942) reported that only seventeen out of 100 women attending a prenatal clinic with their first pregnancy said they had planned it. Of the eighty-three unplanned pregnancies, only eighteen of the women fully accepted it when interviewed, forty-five partially accepted it, and sixteen still found it unacceptable. Thirteen of the women admitted attempting abortions, and sixty-three said they used no contraceptives. 'Under these circumstances, fear of pregnancy was very common and must have played an important role in some of the inadequate sexual adjustments'; these, Thompson thought, were as high as 66 per cent (Thompson 1942:251).

More recent evidence continues to suggest that, although there can be no doubt that the vast majority of girls and women say that they want children at some time in the future, when the time comes, up to 50 per cent are not keen. For example, in 1970, Cobliner reported that 47 per cent of a group of lower-middle-class women in a hospital outside New York, said openly that they did not want the child. But, as Cobliner says, it is rare for a woman to overtly reject the child after birth. Breen (1975) found the figure of unplanned pregnancies to be 41 per cent in a group of fifty women.

But the question as to what actually constitutes a planned pregnancy is not a simple one. A woman who uses no contraception or is lackadaisical about its use, may say that she did not plan her pregnancy. But she is simply saying that she did not take any active steps to become pregnant at that particular time.

One of the few other attempts to find out some of the factors that determine whether a woman wants a child or not, plans a child or not, is that of Grimm and Venet (1966). They studied 124 'normal' middle-class pregnant women to find out what psychological factors were related to the course and outcome of pregnancy. Desire for pregnancy went with higher social class (based on income, education, and occupation), previous children, a relative lack of neurotic symptoms, and satisfaction with the husband and life in general. This relationship between social class and desire for children was also found by Moore and Clautour (1977) in their study of children's attitudes. Is this fairly consistent finding the result of middle-class women having more financial backing that enables them to obtain help with the children, such as nursery schools, help with the housework and so forth?

The class factor must also be borne in mind when considering the many investigations seeking to find out how many children people say they want. Most studies in Europe and North America find that the average desired number is around two, for middle-class samples. This is so for adults in Sweden (Jacobson and Nilsson 1967). Children also have views. For instance, half of a sample of twelve-year-old girls in Britain said they wanted two children, with a range from none to six. The vast majority of these girls wanted children of both sexes, and of those who stated a preference for children of one particular sex, all but one wanted girls (Moore and Clautour 1977).

However, differences become apparent when one looks at subcultures. For example, Vogel and her co-workers (1970) were investigating the sex-role self-concepts of sixty-five single women at a Catholic women's college in the United States, and also asked the women to fill in a Future Plans Questionnaire. One question was 'how many children would your ideal family have?' (women who did not plan to marry were eliminated from the analysis). The number of children desired by these Catholic women was from two to twelve with an average of four. But the Vogel study is particularly interesting in finding that women who had less stereotypically 'feminine' self-concepts (in other words, were high on 'male' attributes) wanted fewer children than did the more 'feminine' women. This parallels the relationship found between sex-role attitudes and completed family size in older women (Clarkson *et al.* 1970). Vogel suggests that the data support the idea that the sex-role self-concepts characteristic of the mothers of small, as opposed to large families, may precede the childbearing period and may be one of the factors determining the number of children a woman eventually does have. Clarkson points out that it is important to check these findings on a non-Catholic population before attempting any generalizations.

Pregnancy: normal or an illness?

'... it appears that one-fifth to one-fourth of all pregnant American women each year define pregnancy as an illness for which they regard the appropriate treatment to be abortion. The "illness" is not just biological but social and economic; and it is not just social, but has a biological basis in fact.'
(Hern 1971:8)

So says Hern pointing to abortion as the modern doctor's dilemma. To have the patient identifying her illness and choosing the treatment 'invades the realm of professional exclusivity, with its attendant prestige and status'. But if women do perceive pregnancy in illness terms, then letting the pregnancy take its course or having an abortion would both be appropriate methods of treatment.

However, Hern points out that most physicians, implicitly or explicitly, regard the female as essentially a reproductive machine. He quotes one physician as defining a woman as 'a uterus surrounded by a supporting organism and a directing personality'. This leads to the view that pregnancy is not only normal but also desirable. And therefore any woman who fails or refuses to become or remain pregnant is pathological. The term 'normal' pregnancy is useful to distinguish those pregnancies without complications from those with. But when the term is used in a non-professional context it reinforces the stereotype of the female as childbearer being more 'normal' than the non-pregnant woman. This then leads to the idea that any woman who wants an abortion needs her head examined as well.

Hern, therefore, suggests that instead of continuing the misguided belief that pregnancy is in itself a normal and desirable state, doctors should consider

'a more accurate view that human pregnancy is an episodic, moderately extended chronic condition with a definable morbidity and mortality risk to which females are uniquely though not uniformly susceptible, and which:
  *is almost entirely preventable through the use of effective contraception, and entirely so through abstinence;
  *when not prevented, is the individual result of a set of species specific bio-social adaptations with a changing significance for species survival;
  *may be defined as an illness requiring medical supervision through (a) cultural traditions, functional or explicit, (b) circumstantial self-definition of illness or (c) individual illness behaviour;
  *may be treated by evacuation of the uterine contents;
  *may be tolerated, sought, and/or valued for the purpose of reproduction;
  *has an excellent prognosis for complete, spontaneous recovery, if managed under careful medical supervision.'
                                                                (Hern 1971 : 9)

We agree with Hern's point that there is a discrepancy between the doctor's view of pregnancy being 'normal' and the woman's view of it as 'abnormal'. For it is abnormal in the sense that most of life is not spent in that state. But nothing is really going to be solved by helping medical practitioners untangle their linguistic disorder and persuading them to regard pregnancy as an illness. For, in many ways, they do regard it as such already in the sense that they are doctors treating women as patients in hospitals and so forth. The problem is to persuade society (and thus doctors) that it is a woman's right to make her own decision, instead of, as at the present time having decision-making taken out of her hands and placed in the doctors'. One other effect of this medical domination is that the woman's real and immediate problems of adjustment are paid no heed to, if someone does actually listen to what she has to say, her problems are used as evidence of possible psychological disturbance.

In a paper delightfully entitled, 'A funny thing happened on my way to the orifice', Scully and Bart (1973) studied gynaecology textbooks to find out if medical attitudes about women have changed over the last quarter of a century. One would hope so after reading Cooke's comment made in 1943 that, 'The fundamental biologic factor in women is the urge of motherhood balanced by the fact that sexual pleasure is entirely secondary or even absent' (Cooke 1943:50). But the sad conclusion from their review is 'no', things have not changed. Since Time (1972) apparently reported that 93.4 per cent of gynaecologists were men, it is important for women to know what their views are about their women patients. Two quotes from Scully and Bart will suffice to make the point. Novak, Jones, and Jones in a 1970 textbook state that:

'The frequency of intercourse depends entirely upon the male sex drive ... The bride should be advised to allow her husband's sex drive to set their pace and she should attempt to gear hers satisfactorily to his. If she finds after several months or years that this is not possible, she is advised to consult her physician as soon as she realizes there is a real problem.'   (Novak, Jones, and Jones 1970:662–3)

Scully and Bart finish with a quote from a textbook by Scott (1968) entitled *The World of a Gynaecologist:*

'If like all human beings he (the gynaecologist) is made in the image of the Almighty, and if he is kind, then his kindness and concern for his patient may provide her with a glimpse of God's image.'   (Scott 1968:25)

Since pregnancy and childbirth are such monumental events and ones that singly differentiate women from men (just as speech differentiates humans from animals), we might hope for a great wealth of research to have been carried out to discover exactly what such experiences mean to women, and what particular factors make adjustment easy for some and difficult if not impossible for others. But, as with women's views on sexual intercourse, our hopes are dashed. There is a considerable body of literature on the abnormal – the unmarried mother, abortions, infertility, sterilization, and so forth – but on the ordinary married woman very little indeed. The questions we want to ask are why she becomes pregnant when she does; or why she chooses not to become pregnant; or why she chooses to become pregnant several times; and what it all means to her in relation to how she conceptualizes herself. But for answers to such questions we will have to wait.

The influence of the 'normality' concept is evident wherever one cares to look in the medical approach to women. For instance, MacIntyre (1973) looked at the type of information General Practitioners asked for and what use they made of the information received, as well as what their unmarried patients thought of the questions. Many of the women expressed surprise at the number of questions relating to past actions. Such questions concerned the number of boyfriends they had had, the type of contraceptives used, and the method of intercourse. MacIntyre points out that these questions are not considered pertinent to married women, but are asked of the unmarried pregnant women so as to build up a crude personality picture of her. Marriage and termination are seen by the General Practitioners as alternatives to the 'problem' of pregnancy in the unmarried woman. For the married woman there is no such 'problem'.

One study has actually looked at whether expectant mothers did perceive their pregnancy as an illness and related this to adjustment (Rosengren 1961). For some, this was the case. Moreover, the women who did regard their pregnancy as akin to a physical illness tended to: (a) expect to be exempt from their normal social obligations; (b) desire to 'recover' as quickly as possible and so return to normal life; (c) feel obliged to be concerned about the organic sensations and possible medical complications during the pregnancy; (d) anticipate pain and suffering as natural concomitants of pregnancy; and (e) feel obliged to play a subordinate role in relation to their medical advisors. Interestingly it seems the woman who felt that her pregnancy was an illness played the part better, since the results showed that her length of labour was significantly longer than her counterpart, who regarded pregnancy as 'normal'. One further finding concerned the role relationship between doctor and patient among the women who regarded themselves as ill. The obstetricians had also been interviewed about their own views of pregnancy. And it was found that those women who saw pregnancy as an illness had significantly longer labour times particularly when attended by a doctor who saw pregnancy as a natural event. The reverse was true with women who saw their pregnancy as a normal event. In fact, where there was doctor/patient incongruency of view, labour took twice as long as it did if there were congruency. But Schwartz (1969) criticizes this conclusion saying:

'I would like to know whether the theories about the nature of childbirth of the doctors and their patients were really congruent, or whether the good deliverers or the nice mothers who let the doctors go home to their own wives earlier by not holding back the baby were those the doctor liked. They may then have felt that the views of the patients were congruent with their own and that was why these patients delivered more rapidly.' (Schwartz 1969:155)

However, it is important to bear in mind that the way an individual perceives his health may be more predictive of how he behaves in the face of illness than the actual medical diagnosis. But most Western physicians are more disease-oriented than patient-oriented, and so few listen to such views.

The concept one has of normality also seems to affect how satisfactory prenatal services are. For instance, Hubert (1974) comments on the ignorance of many women about the process of pregnancy. During their pregnancies, many have only vague

155

ideas about what to expect in terms of symptoms and what to do about these if they experience them. In her study, the women reported feeling that they could not ask questions at the clinics. Apparently, some clinic staff place great emphasis on the 'normal' woman approach and are brisk and practical. But to the women and their mothers this is not a 'normal' event. It is new and sometimes bewildering. So many of the pregnant women turn to their mothers who treat them as if they were marginally ill and support them with many old wives' tales. Hubert comments that:

> 'even where there is excellent medical supervision, and even serious attempts to communicate knowledge there is in fact a wide gap between the fund of knowledge held by the doctors, midwives, and so on, on which they base their concept of the normality of pregnancy, and the limited and very diverse beliefs and ideas held by many of the women they deal with.'
>
> (Hubert 1974:43)

Theories to account for adjustment to pregnancy

As one might expect from the idea that the less one knows about a topic the more one theorizes about it, there are many theories to account for the common reports that women are often anxious or depressed during pregnancy and while in hospital. The range of psychological theories is wide.

Pines (1972), for example, says that 'pregnancy is a crisis point in the search for a female identity ... It implies the end of the woman as an independent single unit and the beginning of the unalterable and irrevocable mother–child relationship' (Pines 1972:333).

Stein (1967) also stresses the association between childbirth and emotional illness, and is in agreement with Hubert's findings that many women become anxious because they feel unable to cope. Stein suggests that:

> 'Childbearing and maternity represent a "change of status" to the woman anticipating a child. This factor is important in giving rise to anxiety and in precipitating reactions of panic

156

because the role and the demands appear overwhelming.'

(Stein 1967:56)

The change of role concerns the task of looking after the child and the feeling of lack of experience, knowledge, and understanding to enable her to do this. *The change of personal status* is mainly in her own eyes because she has to think about the baby before herself; she assumes the name of 'mother' and thus gives away a certain amount of her identity as an individual: 'Individuals who have difficulty in their self evaluations and personal identities in the cultural scheme find it difficult to shift to a new and different role with all of its new responsibilities and demands' (Stein 1967:57).

There is also a *change in marital status* since she becomes a mother and therefore less of a wife. Finally, Stein talks about *change in status within the family pattern*; the woman becomes the mother of a grandchild and so both her parents and her husband's have opinions that need to be given consideration, since she feels an additional responsibility to them, and particularly to her husband's parents.

From a very different theoretical position, Hanford (1968) argues that the pregnant woman is not in the traditional conflict situation since she is approaching a goal about which there is no choice. Hanford feels that the conflict is between the goal towards which she is irrevocably propelled, and her thoughts on the matter. If this is so, then this conflict should decrease as pregnancy proceeds, as she will have time to iron the conflicts out. Symptomatology related to conflict, such as nausea and vomiting, is most frequent in the first three months. Conflict then decreases and so does symptomatology. Hanford here of course assumes that nausea and vomiting are related to conflict. The woman comes to accept the inevitable and the 'system of rewards for being pregnant and being acceptant of pregnancy will have been instituted'. There then follows increasing anxiety as labour approaches, although this is not due to conflict but to realistic fear. Hanford proceeds to theorize about women who do not respond to conflict in the above 'normal' way:

'Women with severe or incapacitating conflict over being pregnant will have much greater difficulty in resolving such conflict. It may be impossible for her to resolve the conflict at all, or if she does, she may do so only at great cost to herself, emotionally and physiologically, and to her child *in utero*.'

(Hanford 1968:1316)

Such women will then have: (a) more severe and prolonged symptoms during early pregnancy; (b) symptoms that will extend into the second trimester; and (c) difficulties and complications. If such conflict can be operationally defined then Hanford's hypothesis can readily be tested.

Rheingold (1964) focuses on a different aspect of the woman's adjustment to pregnancy – what it means for the foetus. He presents a well-elaborated theory on the nature of maternal destructiveness. By this he means:

'Whatever influence the mother exerts upon the foetus, the newborn, the infant, and the young child to which it is susceptible and which tends to interfere with or distort, or provide inadequate supplies for, wholesome personality development.'

(Rheingold 1964:690)

But all is not lost. He sees pregnancy as being:

'our last chance to interrupt the flow of destructiveness from generation to generation. If the pregnant woman is emotionally disturbed (or perhaps even harbors negative attitudes), the foetus is adversely affected, the initial mother–child interaction is stressful, and a life is launched with impaired developmental potentialities. Relief of anxiety in pregnancy is our central concern. It contributes more to the melioration of destructiveness than all other preventive measures combined.'

(Rheingold 1964:708)

He ends his 714 page book with these stirring words: 'When women grow up without dread of their biologic functions and without subversion by feminist and altruistic sentiment, we shall attain the goal of a good life and a secure world in which to live it.' (Rheingold 1964:708). Spoken like a true-blue male psychiatrist whose book is dedicated to 'my women patients'.

It is worth bearing in mind Grimm's words of warning when one is considering theories and research on pregnancy:

'... no one today doubts the considerable influence of social and cultural factors in shaping any kind of psychological reaction. Nor would we expect to find one "psychology of pregnancy" any more than we would speak about the psychology of going to school, marrying, etc.'

(Grimm 1969:130)

Reactions to pregnancy and childbirth

It seems that there can be no rosy illusions that the time of pregnancy and the weeks after are filled with joy and feelings of fulfillment, if we look at what evidence there is about women's views of pregnancy and their reactions to it. Too many studies have found tension, depression, and a multitude of anxieties during the early days as well as later on (see Chapter 10 for details on depression).

The sorry plight of the pregnant woman does not seem to have changed since Thompson carried out a study of women attending his antenatal clinic in 1942.

'... we feel that within the limitations of the positive findings, there are in almost every family of this clinic sampling many problems that are not conducive to a good marital adjustment and to the birth of a healthy, wanted child. These problems often become acute during pregnancy, and they are practical problems which our patients want to bring to a doctor or a nurse, who frequently can give valuable assistance if they will listen to the patient's story. This does not mean that every pregnant woman should be under the care of a psychiatrist, but it does mean that all doctors and nurses who have anything to do with obstetrics should give due attention to the adjustment of the total individual and not focus all attention on the lower half of the torso. Practically, it seems highly desirable that every obstetrical clinic should have at least one full-time psychiatric social worker and that this social worker, as well as the obstetricians and nurses, should have the advisory and consultative services of a psychiatrist.'

(Thompson 1942:256)

159

Several studies since then have sought to determine whether adaptation during pregnancy is related to adaptation in late pregnancy, during labour and in the postpartum period, and what sort of women adjust best. Cohen (1966) started out with:

'the obvious assumption that the more emotionally un-stable women would have the most trouble during their preg-nancies. This turned out to be true in the majority of cases, but to our surprise there was a substantial proportion of quite neurotic women who were no worse or, in some cases, even felt and functioned better during their pregnancies than before or after.' (Cohen 1966:7)

Breen (1975) found a relationship of a rather different sort. Among the fifty women she studied, those with the highest score on a depression questionnaire were those who had the best overall adjustment according to the measures used. (For a dis-cussion of this finding see Chapter 10:173–4.) Others (for ex-ample, Nott *et al.* 1976) have looked at general disturbance and have found a relationship between the degree of distress ex-pressed before and after delivery.

Zemlick and Watson (1953) studied fifteen women attending a 100-bed maternity hospital with a large out-patient obstetrics clinic. They were promised 'individualized care' in return for participation in the project. They were aged between seventeen and thirty and their husbands were mainly skilled and semi-skilled craftsmen. On the basis of ratings of expressed attitudes and various other psychological scales, they reported that anxiety correlated -0.54 with adjustment in labour and de-livery. The more anxiety there was, the less well the women adjusted to labour and delivery.

Zemlick and Watson comment on the marked increase in accepting attitudes after the birth and suggest that this might be due to women repressing their true attitudes when mother-hood becomes a fact. They hypothesize that:

'Mothers who subjectively and objectively display the greatest degree of symptomatology express their rejection through psychosomatic avenues during pregnancy and later exhibit overindulgent, oversolicitous and compulsive

behaviour (maternal persistence) with respect to the child.'
(Zemlick and Watson 1953:582)

It does not seem to occur to authors such as these, that women might just be plain anxious about what is to happen to them. It must be remembered that much of this sort of work is carried out by doctors and nurses who rate their patients according to how they 'think' pregnant women should behave. If they are using the 'normality' concept, then clearly any woman who expresses anxiety or seems depressed is not, in the nurses' and doctors' opinions, behaving normally. Perhaps such biases contribute to the discrepant findings.

Zajicek (1976) carried out a more detailed study. She interviewed fifty-two working-class women in London who were having their first babies. She saw them when they first came to the antenatal clinic, again when seven months pregnant, and then four months after the birth of the baby. She found that women who had psychological problems during pregnancy were three times more likely to have something wrong with them four months after the birth of the child. In fact, as many as 58 per cent of the women had psychiatric or physical problems during pregnancy. Of those who had problems both before and after giving birth, significantly more were under twenty-one years of age.

Zajicek then related pregnancy problems to problems with life in general. She found that those women who had problems in pregnancy and who then had problems at four months after giving birth, were more dissatisfied with life in general and with their husbands in particular. This supports Grimm and Venet's finding (1966).

Breen (1975) used three criteria of adjustment (the obstetricians report, Pitt's depression questionnaire (1968) and a questionnaire designed to compare the woman's view of her own baby with the 'average' baby). These measures showed, among other things, that one-third of the sample of fifty women had difficulty with the baby and/or were depressed, and one-half had some obstetrical difficulties.

Grimm (1969) points out that:

'in our psychologically oriented society, if a woman has a

good deal of nausea during pregnancy or has a terrible labour or is depressed after the baby is born, the first thought of those "in the know" is automatically that she is anxious, neurotic, or rejecting of the child or her femininity.'

(Grimm 1969:140)

But these reactions could be as much to do with physiological stress as to 'healthiness' of personality. Having said that, the general conclusion must be that 'healthiness' of personality is associated with good emotional adjustment to childbearing – but nothing like a one-to-one relationship. It must, however, be remembered that the appropriateness of the woman's reactions are usually being judged by doctors, nurses, or social workers who are all probably operating the 'normality' concept, whereas the patients are perhaps not.

So far, no one seems to have found that the woman's relationship with her father is an important factor in determining whether she will make a 'good' or a 'poor' adaptation to pregnancy, although this is often put forward as an explanation. Cohen (1966) found that problem-free women had good relationships with their mother, but were sometimes in conflict with their father. She was led to conclude from her investigation that the women who best fitted the traditional feminine role being passive and dependent, were inadequate as wives, mothers, and sexual partners. But we are given no data with this report, so cannot assess the validity of these statements.

However, Breen (1975) gives us some further insight into this matter. She obtained a 'femininity' score from the Drawing Completion Test (Franck and Rosen 1948). Those women who adjusted well to childbirth showed a decrease in score from early on in pregnancy to ten weeks after childbirth, while those who were classified as ill-adjusted became more feminine – 'It definitely puts in question the passive picture of the pregnant woman which is generally depicted as "normal" ' (Breen 1975:189).

One of the very surprising findings concerning adjustment appears when a comparison is made between those having their first child and those who already have children. It is always assumed that the first child is more threatening than the experience with subsequent pregnancies. But the opposite seems to be true. Grimm and Venet (1966) found that those not having their first child had shorter labours, but had significantly less desire for the current pregnancy. In fact, the more children the women had already, the less they wanted the present child. These women did not have fewer somatic symptoms during pregnancy either, nor was their adjustment during labour better, nor did they show less depression or a better adaptation postpartum compared with women having their first child.

Cohen (1966) obtained similar results. Fifty per cent more of the women having their second or third child were found to have emotional problems, than those having their first child. Cohen says, 'It looked as though these mothers had learned from experience that pregnancy and child-raising were sources of conflict and dissatisfaction' (Cohen 1966:7).

Cohen's women were middle-class Protestants with moderate financial security and freedom of choice about family size. But Pavenstadt (1965) made a similar study with a lower income group. The women appeared less well adjusted at their third and fourth pregnancy than they had been at their first. One possible explanation for these findings is that it is generally expected that these women need less support than those having their first child, so that they are given relatively little attention.

Rubin (1967) reported some unusual research in which she compared the fantasies of both women having their first child, and those having a child other than their first. The fantasies of both groups were primarily concerned with the self and these increased very much after the start of foetal movement:

'Although some fantasies of a boy child were made these were usually replaced by fantasies, in greater frequency, of a girl child. The child was seen as an extension of self, the wished-for self and the dreaded-self. There were swings to and from wished-for and dreaded-self and usually the more likeable self predominated ... The early romanticized, free-flowing, and idyllic fantasies were replaced by dreaded, body-bound, and gargoyle-type fantasies. Although this was characteristic of pregnancy, the fantasies of self and child continued to sway between these polarities even after the birth of the child, with the only difference between the two periods being a matter of the amount of fantasy, not the content.' (Rubin 1967:242)

The women who were having a child other than their first, reported having less of a fantasy life but it was as rich. There was one fantasy that Rubin reports as universal after the twenty-eighth and thirty-second week : 'In this fantasy the only evidence of a world, outside self and baby, was that of intrusion from without and this always appeared as ominous or dangerous' (Rubin 1967:242). Vulnerability was felt from noises, crowds, strangers, or children.

Ability to cope with the baby

There have been several studies indicating that many women feel unable to cope with their baby. Hubert (1974), for example, found that many women expressed this lack of confidence and saw the whole process as unpleasant and painful. Some felt lonely and thought that someone should have prepared them better for the reality of the event. This feeling of being unable to cope continued for many when they returned home with the baby. They were ill-prepared for this new 'thing' which was supposed to be a little 'person'. 'Instead of a quiet, undemanding, doll-like baby, the new mother is often presented with a squalling, starving animal whose needs are both unpredictable and apparently insatiable' (Hubert 1974:47).

The majority of these women did not want to breastfeed their babies. In fact, only 18 per cent did so. Many reasons were given for not doing so, among which were feelings of embarrassment at doing it in front of others; the general inconvenience it would cause, such as preventing visits to friends and neighbours; while many expressed complete revulsion at the idea. Hubert points out that few of the women studied would have seen anyone breastfeeding, other than the West Indians and Africans in the neighbourhood. These people are often seen breastfeeding in public and are groups with whom these white women would not want to be identified. Hubert comments that, 'It is of course interesting that slightly higher in the social scale some women probably do breastfeed because they wish to be identified with the professional middle-class, among whom breastfeeding is now the fashion' (Hubert 1974:49).

The meaning of pregnancy and childbirth

Why is it that this chapter is so full of alarm and despondency? Perhaps it is simply that one's expectations, coloured by social stereotypes, are that pregnancy and childbirth present no problems. For all these studies are saying is that some women have problems, when they become pregnant, in adjusting to the idea and, thereafter, to the baby – just as some people have problems with marriage, or teenage children. The only difference is that we are led to expect troubles then. All these studies have done is to highlight the fact that pregnancy and childbirth are likely to be times of stress for some women.

We want to end with a brief description of a study that looks in depth at the meaning of pregnancy and childbirth for individual women as well as for a group. In her book *The Birth of a First Child*, Breen (1975) gives us some rare insights into changes that take place in women's views of themselves during pregnancy and after childbirth.

The women were divided up into: (a) a well-adjusted group, showing no disturbance in any measure (22 per cent of the women were in this group); (b) a medium-adjusted group, showing disturbance on one of the three measures (42 per cent of the women were in this group); and (c) an ill-adjusted group showing disturbance on two or all three measures (36 per cent of the women were in this group).

To assess and describe changes in how each woman viewed herself, each completed a repertory grid both early in pregnancy, and ten weeks after giving birth. She was asked first to name a person she considered very motherly and one she considered to be immature. These, together with herself, her mother, father, and husband, and her 'notion of the ideal mother' were the elements for the grid. These elements were then taken three at a time, and constructs were elicited by asking her to see if there were any important ways in which two of the elements were alike and thereby different from the third. To the ten constructs that were elicited in this way, an eleventh was added – the most important quality a mother could have. The elements (people) were then ranked in terms of each of the constructs.

Comparing the first and last grids administered, Breen predicted, and found, that women in the well-adjusted group would see themselves as being more similar to their own mother after the birth of the child. When the data were broken down into whether the mother was seen as 'good' or 'bad' during pregnancy, the expected was the case: after becoming mothers themselves, the women tended to see themselves more like their own mother if she was construed as 'good' and less like her if she were construed as 'bad' in the first instance. There were, in addition, increases in similarity between the self and ideal mother and a dissimilarity between their view of themselves and their husbands.

The picture for the ill-adjusted group is predictably the opposite in many respects. These women became more dissimilar to their mothers and valued themselves less, but they did not see themselves as becoming less like their husbands.

These data are complex, but Breen has given one example of an approach to research which might lead to a better understanding of what pregnancy actually means in the life of a woman.

TEN

Women and their mental health

Rates of ill-health

It is a common finding that women exceed men in the rate of anxiety neurosis, depression, and other psychiatric disorders. There is even a special heading in the *Yearbook of Neurology, Psychiatry and Neurosurgery* describing a syndrome called 'Housewife's Disease' (1964–5). Many studies give actual rates. For example, Gove and Tudor (1973) found that for every million people in the United States, 400 men and 487 women were admitted to mental hospital for the first time. But psychiatric care in general hospitals showed an even greater sex discrepancy – 1,775 men and 3,402 women. British data can be seen in *Table 7*. Community surveys have also found more women being mentally ill than men (see, for example, Leighton *et al*. 1963). It also appears that, with increasing education, the rate of psychiatric symptoms decreases for men but not for women (see Ödegärd 1963).

Change in rate is also found by Landau (1973). Women

outnumber men in terms of in-patient and out-patient psychiatric care, and the difference has been on the increase in the last thirty years. But it is not an inevitable and universal finding that women are more susceptible to mental problems than men. Niskanen, Tamminen, and Achte (1974) looked at sex and duration of stay in the Psychiatric Clinic of the Helsinki

Table 7 Admissions by sex and diagnostic group mental illness hospitals and units in England and Wales in 1970.

	male	female	total
all diagnoses	72,098	104,065	176,163
schizophrenia, schizo-affective disorders, and paranoia	17,088	18,669	35,757
depressive psychoses, involutional melancholia	7,597	17,824	25,421
psychoses of the senium	3,444	7,295	10,739
psychoneuroses	8,326	16,336	24,662

(Source: *Health and Personal Social Services Statistics for England and Wales*, 1972.)

University Central Hospital in Finland over the last 130 years. Overall, 44 per cent women and 56 per cent men were inhabitants, and in nearly all decades there were more men than women.

Social factors and ill-health

Some evidence suggests that this differential rate of psychiatric disorder between men and women may be a sociological phenomenon in part at least. Leighton and her co-workers (1963) found what other North American and British community studies had found – higher rates of disorder for women than for men in general. However, in this massive study they were able to subdivide their samples. On the one hand they looked at three 'disintegrating' communities undergoing a period of severe economic depression. These were compared with two communities 'outstandingly high in integration'. Not only did the depressed communities yield a higher than average rate of psychological disorder generally, but the men had higher rates

168

than the women. The well-integrated communities had lower rates in general as might be expected. But the two well-integrated communities were studied separately. In the close-knit French community the rates for women were lower than those for men, whereas in the English community (socially more loosely structured), the rates for women were higher than for men. The importance of social factors on the occurrence of psychological disorders can also be found in Brown, Bhrolchain, and Harris's work (1975).

Social class and ill-health

It is the relationship between social class and psychiatric disorder with which Brown, Bhrolchain, and Harris (1975) are primarily concerned. They are of the opinion that such disturbance is largely a social phenomenon and, as such, some understanding of the workings of society can be gained by a study of the distribution of such disturbances. The authors are particularly concerned with the role of adverse life events in the occurrence of psychiatric disorder.

They studied two groups of women living in a London borough, aged between sixteen and sixty-five years. The first group consisted of 114 women who were being treated as either in- or out-patients diagnosed as suffering from depression starting during the year prior to interview. The second group consisted of 220 women randomly selected from the same district. In this latter group, 16 per cent were judged to have had a definite psychiatric disorder within the three months prior to interview. But they were considered to be less disturbed than those receiving treatment. All were suffering from disorders of mood. Another 20 per cent had definite symptoms, but would only rarely be expected to be seen in a psychiatric out-patient clinic.

The authors found that working-class women were about five times more likely to develop psychiatric disorders than were middle-class women, when confronted with a severe life event or major difficulty (30 per cent and 6 per cent respectively). Four factors lead to an increased probability of a psychiatric problem developing in such circumstances: lack of an intimate relationship, lack of a job, loss of the woman's own mother in early childhood, and having three or more children living at home. These are more common with working-class women and are taken to explain the class difference in vulnerability. They also just have more major crises in their lives, be it threats of eviction, problems with children or ill-health, as well as the normal deaths and disasters that affect everyone. In fact, 26 per cent of the total community sample and 61 per cent of the patient sample had had a severely threatening event in an average nine-month period before interview (for the community sample) and at onset of the depression (for the patient sample). But it seems that the working-class woman with a child under the age of six is particularly at risk.

Overall, 10 per cent of the middle-class women and 25 per cent of the working-class women who were not patients were judged to be suffering from some form of chronic psychiatric complaint; 43 per cent of these had major housing problems. Brown comments that '. . . hardly any of the women whom we considered in the present study to be psychiatrically disturbed had seen a psychiatrist – scarcely half had seen a medical practitioner'. Again, it is the working-class women who are less likely to seek treatment.

Another type of class difference was noted by Weissman and Paykel (1974) when they compared a group of forty 'normal' women with forty depressed women. They concluded that people treating depressed women 'should beware of expecting wider social participation, assertiveness in marriage, and independence from extended family, which are norms of middle-class, upwardly mobile professionals but may not be appropriate for all patients' (Weissman and Paykel 1974:218). With most 'treaters' being middle-class and the majority of depressed women being working-class, this cautionary note is very relevant. But Bart (1971) came to the conclusion from her study that it was the middle-class woman who was more likely to become depressed. However, Brown, Bhrolchain, and Harris's study suggests one explanation for these discrepant findings: it may be because the middle-class woman is more likely to seek psychiatric help.

(a) *In general*. Apart from 'Housewife's Disease', by far the greatest cause of women seeking treatment is depression. For instance, Silverman (1968) states that 'There appear to be no exceptions to the generalization that depression is more common in women than in men, whether it is the feeling of depression, neurotic depression, or depressive psychosis' (Silverman 1968:73). However, this is not reflected in the suicide rates. In fact, more men than women commit suicide (see, for example, Ross and Kreitman 1975). Yet this does not necessarily mean women are less distressed than men since women are much more likely to attempt suicide (see Stengel 1972). But bare figures often do not give the whole picture. There is some evidence that the rate of suicide among women has been on the increase in recent years but there has been no such increase among men. Housewives seem to be particularly at risk. Brown, Bhrolchain, and Harris (1975) succeeded in identifying four factors which resulted in housewives becoming depressed, when faced with a serious life event or difficulty. These were loss of mother in childhood, three or more children aged under fourteen living at home, lack of an intimate confiding relationship with a husband or boyfriend, and lack of full- or part-time work. The authors saw the intimacy factor as reflecting the amount of emotional support and general level of satisfaction the husband gives his wife 'in her role of mother and housewife'. They likewise discuss the role played by having a job in reducing the likelihood of psychiatric disturbance after some major disrupting event, and think that it may be related to an increase in self-esteem and comments:

'... the circumstances implied by at least three of the vulnerability factors generate a sense of failure and dissatisfaction in meeting internalised expectations of being a good mother and wife, and that this in turn leads to chronically low self-esteem, leaving the woman particularly vulnerable to the effects of loss.'

(Brown, Bhrolchain, and Harris 1975:23)

The same conclusion concerning the 'protective' nature of a

171

job was reached by Weissman and Paykel (1974) in their study of forty depressed American women. They also reported that these depressed women showed most impairment and caused most friction, inside the home, but many managed to continue working successfully outside the home, in spite of being fairly seriously depressed.

In a very extensive study of 1,545 people in America, of whom 908 were women, Warheit, Holzer, and Schwab (1973) looked at what they called 'negative evaluations and attitudes about the future'. These negative attitudes were ascertained through statements and questions such as : 'When things don't turn out, how often would you say you blame yourself?' and 'Life has changed so much in our modern world that people are powerless to control their own lives'. On the basis of responses to questions such as these, and to questionnaires covering bodily complaints, altered patterns of eating, sleeping, and so forth, the authors concluded : 'The data reported in this paper indicate that blacks, females, the aged, the poor, and those with the least formal education had the highest rates of depressive symtom-atology' (Warheit, Holzer, and Schwab 1973 : 297).

Depression does tend to occur considerably more often in women than in men throughout their life span in Western cultures, though it is true that the research has mainly been concerned with depression in relation to childbirth and ageing. Chesler (1972) sees the former as a way of 'keeping a deadly faith with their "feminine" role' (Chesler 1972 : 45). She cites Friedman's findings (1970) that depressed women in hospital express even less verbal hostility and aggression than do non-depressed women.

(b) *At childbirth*. All is not rosy for women even at the time when everyone thinks she should be at her happiest – having given birth to her infant. There is even some evidence that mothers are generally more susceptible to physical and psychological disorders, than married women who are childless (Malmquist and Kaj 1971). The general confusion and unhappiness of many women during their pregnancies has been discussed in Chapter 9, but an alarming number of women become acutely depressed after childbirth, especially in the first three months. The actual numbers involved are in dispute, often because of problems of definition – for instance, how long the postpartum period is considered to be. However, a number of studies have shown a connection between childbearing and depression. For example, in an early study, Pugh *et al.* (1963) calculated the number of first admissions to public and private mental hospitals that would be expected on the basis of past figures, among women of childbearing age in Massachusetts in 1950. This was compared with the number observed. There were significantly fewer admissions for all types of psychiatric disorder in pregnant women. But for the nine-month period after childbirth there were significantly more, especially during the first three months.

If it is really so that more women become depressed after childbirth than would be expected for women of their age, what could be the reason? Here is a fertile breeding ground for theories because there seem to be few facts. Part of the picture may be supplied by Breen (1975). She found that, of the women who did not become depressed, 61 per cent had boys whereas only 17 per cent of the depressed women were 'so fortunate'. Breen suggests that we need not look to Freud's theory that women compensate for their lack of a penis by having a son, but rather take his idea that a mother's relationship with her son is the one most lacking in conflict that there is.

Pitt (1968) however, did not find such a relationship between depression and the sex of the child. But his sample included women who were having a child other than their first – some had boys already. Pitt looks at the occurrence of depression. both mild and severe, following childbirth, and cites Robin (1962) as having reported that weeping occurs in up to 80 per cent of women. However, a very much more severe form of depression can follow childbirth. Pitt says this puerperal depression may occur in up to one in every 500 births.

Pitt studied 305 pregnant women and interviewed and tested them again after childbirth. While 50 per cent could be regarded as mildly depressed in that they suffered from 'the blues' while in hospital, an alarming 10·8 per cent were depressed for a longer period. 'It was after the return home that depression was always most evident, chiefly as tearfulness, despondency, feelings of inadequacy and inability to cope – particularly with the baby' (Pitt 1968 : 1327). Anxiety was often present but was not usually justified by the state of the baby's health. Pitt comments that this depression must have been considered normal by the women and their relatives since only five of the thirty-three were receiving treatment from their GPs. Some were, however, 'getting help indirectly by discussing anxieties about their babies with G.P.'s, health visitors or at local Welfare Clinics' (Pitt 1968 : 1328).

These figures can be compared with those of Breen (1975), who used the same questionnaire. Among her fifty women, she found 21 per cent to be depressed after childbirth. Breen gives three possible reasons why there should be such a difference between her group and Pitt's: her group filled out the questionnaire at home rather than in hospital; Pitt's group contained women who were not having their first child whereas her women were; and Pitt tested his group six to eight weeks after giving birth compared with her ten to fifteen weeks.

Pitt comments that, despite the apparent mildness of the depression, 43 per cent had not substantially improved after one year. This was 4 per cent of the total sample. He argued that depression following childbirth may be much more extensive than previous studies have lead one to believe, since most investigators study the numbers of women admitted to hospital. This finding that many depressed women do not seek medical help is in accord with that of Brown, Bhrolchain, and Harris (1975).

Pitt's depression score was one of the criteria Breen used to divide her group up into well-adjusted, medium-adjusted, and ill-adjusted.

It is interesting that the raw data show that the well-adjusted group had a significantly higher mean depression score than the ill-adjusted group during pregnancy and a significantly lower one after delivery. Her principal components analysis of the questionnaire leads her to suggest that the well-adjusted women were, among other things, those who could express feelings of anxiety and insecurity during pregnancy. This fits nicely with Janis's notion (1971) of, 'the work of worrying'. Adjustment to a situation comes through the person being able to face a situation realistically and to have a good think about the worrying aspects. This means paying no attention to the medical advice, 'don't worry, it'll all be over soon'. Relating to content, she found that during pregnancy more than half the women indicated on the questionnaire that they woke up easily, cried easily, had less desire for sex, and had not enough energy. After delivery more than half were still easily woken up, but now more were worried about their looks.

Similar results were found in a Swedish study by Jacobson and Nilsson in 1967. These authors looked at the psychiatric and gynaecological symptoms shown by 861 women after they gave birth to their babies, in a hospital in the south of Sweden. Of particular interest is the fact that the number of psychiatric symptoms increased as the number of children the woman had, increased.

The women reported such things as irritability, difficulty in relaxing, and pessimism about the future. While we may not all agree that these are 'symptoms' in the medical sense, they do seem to add to the picture that having the home filled with bonny bouncing babies and growing children is not what all women consider to be the ultimate in happiness. This evidence, as in Chapter 9, shows that the more children a woman had, the less good her adjustment to another pregnancy was likely to be.

(c) *In middle age.* Bart (1971) came to the conclusion that menopausal depression is more likely to be related to psychological stress than to physiological changes. In one part of her study she looked at the files containing data from thirty societies and analysed six of them intensively. The evidence she amassed suggests that depression occurring in the years forty to forty-five is related to a decrease in status, leading to a diminution in self-esteem.

She then looked at the records of 533 women ranging from forty to fifty-nine years in five hospitals in Los Angeles. The hospitals ranged from the 'upper-class private' to the 'State'. None of the women she studied had had a previous history of psychiatric illness. She found that it was the housewives who had been over-protective to children now no longer at home, who were most likely to become depressed. The highest rate was among Jewish women, and it is for these women that the loss of the maternal role is considered to be most disrupting. 'Because the most important roles for women in our society are the roles of wife and mother, the loss of either of these roles might result in a loss of self-esteem – in the feeling of worthlessness and uselessness that characterizes depressives' (Bart 1971 : 172).

To support this view, Bart cites her finding that black women have a lower rate of depression than white women. She says that it is rare for the black woman to suffer from maternal role loss since the social pattern is often one in which 'granny' looks after the children while mother goes out to work. Also, since the majority of black women in America work, it is possible that they will not develop such very restricted maternal role-concepts. However, she realistically points out that the low figure obtained for depression in black women could also be the result of the hospitals' reluctance to admit them. Also, since many black women would be categorized as working-class, they would be less likely to seek psychiatric help than their white middle-class counterparts. It is also possible, although there is no evidence for this, that working-class black people are less likely to seek help than white working-class people in the United States, because of the differing availability of services.

Bart then went on to interview twenty women while they were still in hospital. She found they confirmed everything her previous data had led her to believe. Her conclusion is that it is not the 'masculine' women, so beloved of the psychoanalyst, who are likely to meet trouble at the time of the menopause, but rather 'it is the women who assume the traditional feminine role – who are housewives, who stay married to their husbands, who are not overly aggressive, in short who "buy" the traditional norms – who respond with depression when their children leave' (Bart 1971 : 184).

It has long been thought that hysterectomy must increase the likelihood of a woman becoming depressed. The argument seems reasonable. If a woman has devoted all her life to her home, children, and husband, then what is more likely than that she become depressed at the thought of no longer being able to fulfill her 'natural' role. But Silverman (1968) cites an unpublished series of studies (National Institute of Mental Health 1966) in which it was shown that rates of mental illness of any sort in women who had a hysterectomy before the age of forty were no higher than for other women. When a difference was found, those who had hysterectomies also had prior histories of mental illness. There is no evidence that women of child-bearing age are so upset by having their most vital organ removed that they complain of, or have to receive treatment for, depression. We have, however, no evidence about the effects of hysterectomies in women past childbearing age. It is possible that the operation may increase the tendency to depression.

Specific disorders

Studies of depressed women form the bulk of the available literature on those labelled as being psychiatrically disturbed. But there have been a few studies looking at specific disorders.

(a) *Alcoholism*. Litman's study of alcoholism (1975) is an example of the type of approach that looks at what people think of 'them' rather than asking 'them' what they think of 'themselves'. For instance, she does not ask the women how their drinking fits in with their view of life in general and their role in the family in particular. Perhaps they, like Hoy's alcoholic men (1973), do not see themselves as alcoholics; but rather as people who need a little help to carry on their onerous or tedious job of being wife and mother.

But Wilsnack (1973) got nearer the mark by attempting to study the sex-role identity of twenty-eight female alcoholics in comparison with a group of women of equivalent age, education, and socio-economic status. She points out that the clinical view of such people is that they do not have a well-developed female sex-role identity. She cites clinicians describing female alcoholics as having 'masculine identifications' or as 'identifying with the father'. Could it be that the clinician cannot conceive of a feminine female indulging in such traditionally masculine behaviour? Her survey of the literature indicates that the alcoholic woman's family background often consists of a domineering and emotionally-distant mother, and a weak and passive father. 'This parental combination, in which both parents deviate from normal sex-role behaviour, does not seem favourable

177

for the daughter's development of a secure, positive feminine identification' (Wilsnack 1973:253). But this argument must be set against other evidence that shows non-disturbed women seeing themselves as having father-like qualities (for example, Liftshitz 1976). In fact, Sperlinger's findings (1971) suggest that it is more 'normal' for women to see themselves like their fathers than their mothers. He studied a group of women receiving treatment for depression from their GPs. When depressed, the women saw themselves more like their mothers than their fathers. But, when they improved, they changed to see themselves as being more like their fathers and in that were similar to his group of non-depressed women.

In her own study (1973), Wilsnack uses the three-tier model of sex-role identity described by McClelland and Watt (1968). First, we have gender identity which represents our unconscious feelings about masculinity–femininity; next comes sex-role style, which develops later but is still relatively unconscious; and lastly there are sex-typed attitudes and interests, which are the conscious feelings about masculinity–femininity. Wilsnack's expectation was that there would be no difference between the alcoholic women and the control group of women in conscious identification, but that the alcoholics would be somewhat more masculine on the sex-role style level. No predictions were made about the unconscious level.

A couple of the tests used by Wilsnack are worth reporting here as examples of the extraordinary ideas some psychologists have about what women should think. One test of conscious femininity is a set of nine true–false items that McClelland and Watt had used previously. To us the most interesting ones were:

Traditional femininity item	Typical feminine response
I used to keep a diary	true
I like to cook	true
I pray several times a week	true
I would like to be a florist	true
I am not afraid of mice	false
I am not afraid of fire	false

The other test worth recording is that designed to measure role-preference. In this test, the person is asked to choose which role from each of the following pairs he/she would like to perform in a play or pageant.

old grandfather	vs.	old grandmother
angel	vs.	Lord
scientist	vs.	fashion designer
sister	vs.	brother
Devil	vs.	witch
secretary	vs.	policeman
cow	vs.	bull

While it is possible to see the stereotype at work in the mind of the test constructors, in the choice between a heavenly angel and dominant Lord, a placid cow or aggressive bull, the choice between a Devil and Witch seems particularly inappropriate. But perhaps the American view of witches differs markedly from the hag on the broomstick of European mythology.

The results with the alcoholic women showed them not to be less feminine on the conscious femininity tests. In fact, they were construed as being more feminine in the sense that they would have liked to have had more children than would the control group (4.15 and 2.94 respectively). This may be partly due to the fact that they actually had fewer children (1.70) compared with the average (2.61). Taking this research at face value, we have now come across three examples of excessive femininity being related to psychological disturbance: in pregnancy (Cohen 1966), in the depression of middle age (Bart 1971), and now in alcoholics (Wilsnack 1973). But it is always important, when assessing results, to bear in mind the methods used to obtain them.

However, on the measure of sex-role identity, the alcoholic women were significantly more 'masculine' than the controls. They were 'masculine' in that they said they did not 'like to accept the leadership of someone else in deciding what the group is going to do' and they did think that 'it is very important to do your best in all situations'. On the face of it, these women were simply asking to be allowed to be individuals rather than one of the crowd. Wilsnack comments that they:

'were not only "masculine" and assertive on a measure of

> sex-role style. They were also more masculine than the con-
> trols – and more masculine than groups of female high school
> students and female drug abusers – on the Franck test, a
> measure which appears to tap an unconscious preverbal level
> of sex-role identity.'   (Wilsnack 1973:258)

She also raises the point that since these women are typically
feminine or even supra-feminine consciously, their more masculine sex-role identity may give rise to insecurity as to their
adequacy as women.

Could she be right but for different reasons? McClelland and
Watt (1968) also found evidence (if we take their tests at face
value) that female schizophrenics 'tend to react in a more assertive manner like normal males, and male schizophrenics in a
more sensitive manner like normal females ... The inclination
of female schizophrenics toward assertive story sequences is
matched by a similar inclination in career women ...'
(McClelland and Watt 1968:226). That career women are at risk
is suggested by Ödegärd's study (1963) of Norwegians who were
admitted to hospital up to twenty-five years after graduation.
Not only was there a higher rate among women than men, but
whereas the first admissions of male graduates approximated
that for males in general, the rate for women graduates was
significantly higher than for the female population at large.

Thus career women, drug abusers, alcoholics, and schizophrenics are all giving evidence that they are more 'masculine'
(that is, they are prepared to have their say). But some psychologically disturbed women also seem to be ultra-feminine.
Whichever the case may be, for some women the failure to find
the right balance seems to be partly due to the stereotype which,
instead of acting as a guideline, has become a prescriptive norm.

(b) *Weight disorders*. A fairly successful way in which to
counter the stereotype is to grossly change one's physical shape
by radically over- or under-eating. Anyone who becomes abnormally under-weight may be dubbed as suffering from anorexia
nervosa, and abnormally over-weight as suffering from obesity.
Both are regarded as neurotic disorders. Anorexia nervosa is
seen by Crisp (1970) as a way of denying one's femininity. The
disorder usually occurs in young women, often starting in their

teens, and results, among other things, in a disruption of the menstrual cycle and poor development of breasts.

There is very little information concerning the views men or women have of themselves and their shapes; much more usual are descriptive accounts of what each thinks of the opposite sex. But Fransella and Crisp (1974) tried to gain some insight into the problem by seeking attitudes to weight from twenty women of normal weight who had no psychiatric history; twenty women of normal weight who were in a psychiatric hospital with some kind of neurotic disorder; and twelve women who were in hospital diagnosed as suffering from anorexia nervosa.

The method for assessing attitudes was repertory grid technique (described in Chapter 4). The women were required to name people they knew who fitted certain role titles (such as a person I admire, a person I dislike, a person who makes me anxious or uneasy), together with mother, father, and themselves as they see themselves now (either over- or under-weight), and themselves as they would be if they were a normal weight. These people and the various 'selves' were ranked again and again in relation to certain constructs (such as sexually attractive, an ideal weight, and so forth).

The women of normal weight saw themselves, as people, more or less as they would like to be and as sexually attractive. And they were reasonably satisfied with their present weight when it was compared with being much fatter. But both they and the neurotic groups expressed general dissatisfaction with their present weights, these being significantly higher than their expressed ideal weights. They were weight conscious. The neurotic group agreed with the others that fatness is 'bad', but they did not see themselves as being like their ideal self, nor as being particularly sexually attractive. This discrepancy between the view of self and ideal self is what one is now led to expect in those diagnosed as neurotic.

The anorexic women, coming for treatment grossly underweight, provide a confusing picture. But two things are clear. One is that *mother* is seen very much in terms of their ideal self. The other is that they see people of normal weight as being sexually attractive which they, when thin, are not. This

181

preoccupation with *mother* came up again in a study of a group of eight obese women. They saw themselves at, twenty stone say, as being like their mother. But they would not be like her if they were a normal weight. Since the way they saw themselves ideally was also related to being like mother, it is reasonable to suppose that this may be one of the factors leading them to maintain their over-weight. As to being sexually attractive, these obese women were realistic in not seeing themselves as that now, but their ideal self was not seen as sexually attractive either.

Chetwynd, Stewart, and Powell (1974) summarized studies using repertory grid technique carried out with groups of men and women of various ages, and of various social, occupational, and cultural groups, regarding their attitudes to the obese. Obesity was considered by nearly all groups of people as undesirable. But in addition to this, the authors found that the women were more likely to see the obese women as wives (and possibly mothers) than were the men. The women also tended to see obese people as kinder, more influential, and prudish, than did the men. The 'influential' construct is an interesting one, as if sheer size might give one power. But perhaps this is not such a strange idea after all.

Before leaving physical attributes and women's perceptions of them, there is a relevant study on children's perceptions of abnormalities, including obesity. Richardson and his colleagues, (1961) studied 530 boys and 513 girls from wealthy United States families. He used a form of grid in which he was concerned to understand their attitudes to physical handicaps. These children aged between five and twelve were asked to rank pictures of children with disabilities. The pictures were first ranked from 'I like best' to 'I like least' by the children, and then the parents did the same 'as if' their children were doing the ranking.

The picture of the child with no handicap was universally preferred to all the other children, no matter what their handicap was. Both boys and girls liked the obese child the least, with one exception. The exception was the female twelfth graders for whom the child with a facial disfigurement was liked least. By the end of high school, the rank order preference of boys and girls was almost identical with that of their parents. Boys dislike functional disabilities and girls cosmetic ones. Thus obesity is considered undesirable by children and adults alike. Moreover, in the Richardson study we have a demonstration that the female preoccupation with facial attractiveness and the male focus on athletic ability develop in childhood. Something we all know but until it is spelt out in this way, it is not possible to start investigating the whys, hows, and wherefores.

Possible reasons for differential sex fates in psychological disturbance

If we accept as incontrovertible the evidence that women are more likely to seek psychological treatment than men and may, in fact, be more likely to become psychologically disturbed, then it is reasonable to ask why this is so. We accept that there is no unequivocal evidence that women are constitutionally more likely to become depressed. So we can look to psychological and sociological explanations.

(a) *Social role and its relation to mental health.* For the majority of women, the role of mother and housewife is ill-defined as well as insufficient. How many times do women describe themselves as 'just a housewife'? Being a housewife means little more than adjusting to day-to-day events which, in the long term are trivial, but which appear important at the time. If the wife focuses on motherhood then she will retire in her early forties. If she prides herself on her home, then she makes work for herself. It has been shown that even with the increase in labour-saving devices now available, women spend just as long doing the housework. If women work outside the home, then it seems they do not perceive this as so important as the work of their husbands. For instance, Epstein (1970) found that working women saw their job mainly as a supplement to the family budget. And Rose (1951) reported that college women saw their careers in terms of what the men would do, whereas the men perceived their careers in terms of their own needs. Also, it should be borne in mind that the majority of men have at least two major roles, that defined by their job and that of husband and 'head of the house'.

One important part of the background that must not be overlooked is that working women have an additional stress to contend with, that of working many more hours per day than men do, since their jobs are usually in addition to keeping the house running smoothly. But perhaps the most stressful aspect for the housewife, working or not, is the lack of real control she has over events. This has all been discussed in some detail in Chapters 1 and 2, but here we are interested in its possible relation to mental ill-health. Additional evidence that women perceive themselves as relatively powerless to control events comes from Olsen (1969). He asked young couples expecting babies questions about who would make decisions in certain situations. He then set up experimental situations to determine exactly who did in fact make the decisions. He found that 73 per cent of the husbands overestimated their role in decision making and 70 per cent of the women underestimated their power.

This link between how a person perceives himself and another's observation of what he actually does is important. If you consider yourself dominating and think this is as you should be, but see yourself and are observed to behave in a submissive way, this may be viewed as 'good' by the observer, but as 'bad' by yourself. It will give rise to disquiet within yourself. We must therefore assume that it matters if women perceive themselves as relatively powerless or helpless in the face of life's events. Seligman (1975) published his account of the possible consequences of such an outlook on life in his book entitled *Helplessness*. He is saying that if one comes to the conclusion that life controls her rather than *vice versa*, then she is likely to become depressed. 'The cause of depression is the belief that action is futile.'

Against a background of ill-defined roles, lack of control over events, and the generally unstructured life of the non-working woman, it is perhaps not surprising that she does not question her life and is inclined to worry over the events that are outside her control. Because, not only does she have more time available to worry but she has more to worry about, since she may see many things as being outside her control. Before the woman reader starts shouting and gnashing her teeth, we are aware that there is a great deal of physical work to do around the home and outside it, but much of it is of mind-bending simplicity – washing up, mending, sweeping. All of which encourage the mind to wander in fantasy-land, both worrying and pleasurable.

There is very little research on the psychological well-being of women, but one study suggests that there is a tendency for women to worry more than men. Bradburn and Caplovitz (1965) interviewed a large number of people in America during the Cuban crisis. One thing they found was that women up to the age of sixty were more likely to be highly worried by the situation than men. This was, to some extent, related to the presence of children in the household – the presence of children meaning more worrying. Added to this was the fact that the men were much better informed than the women. The authors suggest that these findings may partly result from men being able to discuss the problems with others at work and so deal with their anxieties.

But why is it that the full-time housewives were not as well informed? On the face of it, they should have been better informed if anything. They should have had more time to read, listen to radio and television commentaries, and to discuss it with their friends. Perhaps it is the helplessness syndrome operating again. 'Men make decisions', so what really is the point of making oneself better informed? So they go on worrying.

Another group of women who are suspected of having underlying conflicts are those who take up careers. This of course is not always the case, but Gump (1972) found that when a college woman saw her future career as being in conflict with herself as a wife and mother, she was less happy.

Another consequence of the role subscribed for women is Horner's 'fear of success' (1968, 1970, 1972, see Chapter 6). Hoffman (1974a) repeated the essentials of Horner's original study to find out exactly what it is that women fear. But she came up with no answers, finding simply that 65 per cent of college women in America were anxious about succeeding. This figure is substantially the same as Horner's original obtained in 1968, suggesting that little has changed in women's attitudes to career training over the last ten years. What was interesting was that 77 per cent of the male students were also anxious about success.

(b) *Sex-role stereotypes and clinical diagnosis.* It appears that about 90 per cent of psychiatrists (in the United States anyway) and an estimated 85 per cent of clinical psychologists are men (Chesler 1972). Is this a factor that may help explain why more women are seen as having psychological problems than men?

Broverman and her co-workers (1970) argued that behaviours regarded as socially desirable are positively related to ratings of normality as opposed to abnormality, health versus sickness, and adjustment. Since men's stereotypic behaviours are rated as more socially desirable than women's, clinicians may rate women's behaviours differently from men's. What may be considered as pathological in one sex may not be seen as such in the other.

For their study they divided seventy-nine medical and non-medical clinicians, aged between twenty-three and fifty-five, into three groups. One filled out the Rosenkrantz Sex-Role Questionnaire according to the instructions 'think of normal, adult men and then indicate on each item the pole to which a mature, healthy, socially competent adult man would be closer'. The second group were given 'female' instructions and the third group were told to fill out the questionnaire to describe a '... healthy, mature, socially competent adult person'.

Apart from getting male and female stereotype scores, there was also a health score. This was based on the assumption that, when no sex was specified, the ratings would reflect ideal, standard, healthy behaviours. So the male and female health scores would be the number of poles on which there was agreement between the ideal and the typical healthy man or woman. No difference was found between male and female clinicians as to what they thought constituted the healthy male and the healthy female. But the clinicians considered socially desirable masculine characteristics as healthier for men than for women. Only seven out of the eleven socially desirable feminine characteristics are seen as more healthy for women than for men.

Broverman goes on to point out that this is not as innocuous as it appears when one looks at the specific items. Healthy women differ from healthy men in the view of male and female clinicians by being more submissive, less independent, less adventurous, more easily influenced, less aggressive, less competitive, more excitable in minor crises, having their feelings more easily hurt, being more emotional, more conceited about their appearance, and less objective. They are of the opinion that this is a powerful negative assessment of women and 'seems a most unusual way of describing any mature, healthy individual' (Broverman *et al.* 1970:5).

There is support for this in the finding that male health concepts do not differ significantly from the ideal ones, whereas female health concepts do. This means that the clinicians were much less likely to attribute 'health' concepts to a woman than they were to a man. '. . . a double standard of health is actually applied only to men, while healthy women are perceived as significantly less healthy by adult standards' (Broverman *et al.* 1970:5). Nowacki and Poe (1973) carried out Broverman's experiment again, this time with psychology students. Another difference was that they used an independent measure of mental health. On both the Sex-Role Questionnaire and the mental health scale, there were significant discrepancies between the ratings for the healthy male and the healthy female. The fact that the differences were again found using an independent mental health measure shows that they are not simply to be found on the Sex-Role Questionnaire. Similarly, Fabrikant (1974) reported that male therapists rated 70 per cent of female concepts as negative whereas they rated 71 per cent of male concepts as positive; women therapists were not far behind with 68 per cent and 67 per cent respectively. It does seem reasonable to conclude from this that more women than men are diagnosed as psychologically disturbed because they are halfway there already! But the contrary evidence and criticisms given by Stricker (1977) indicate we still have much to learn on this topic.

(c) *Willingness to report symptoms.* We take as our starting point the work of Phillips and Segal (1969) who interviewed 153 women and 149 men in a small New England community. The

187

people were all married and aged between twenty-one and fifty years. The reason for all this hard work was to test the hypothesis that among groups of men and women reporting similar numbers of physical illnesses, women will report more psychiatric symptoms than will men. Women may think it more socially acceptable for them to report such problems. The authors used the measuring instrument for identifying psychiatric symptoms as had Gove and Tudor (1973). These latter investigators had rejected the 'willingness to respond' hypothesis but gave no data to support their rejection.

There is nothing inherently deviant in two people holding hands in public. But society and 'experts' categorize it as such if the two people happen to be men. Similar sex norms apply to expressive behaviour. Men have the 'stiff upper lip', and have 'to grin and bear it', whereas the woman is allowed 'to let her hair down'. Phillips and Segal argue that the social expectation to which men conform is one which focuses on self-control, and which sees illness as a feminine characteristic.

Both men and women reported, on average, similar numbers of physical disorders. But for women the number of psychological complaints increased as the number of physical complaints increased. Although it is not possible to make a direct comparison, this could be considered to support Brown, Bhrolchain, and Harris's finding (1975) that depression in women was related to the occurrence of a major difficulty or severe events. A series of physical disorders could be categorized as a major difficulty, particularly in the United States where illness can impose severe financial strain. But Phillips and Segal do not break their data down into social classes. They conclude that their findings support those of other workers '... by showing that under roughly equal circumstances of objective physical illness, women are more likely than men to report feelings and behaviour that are seen by mental health investigators as signs of psychiatric disturbance' (Phillips and Segal 1969:63).

But Clancy and Gove (1974) were not impressed by the work of Phillips and Segal. 'Although their article is replete with data tangentially related to their argument, they have no data bearing directly on this main premise' (Clancy and Gove 1974:205). Clancy and Gove aimed to put this right. They argued that the more socially undesirable the items in scales are, the less likely one is to acknowledge having such behaviour, and *vice versa*. If such is really the case, then women should construe the items in the Langner Scale (1962) used in the previous studies as less undesirable than men should and so feel freer to report psychiatric symptoms. The authors also contend that there are two other types of bias likely to influence responses on the Langner Scale. These are 'need for approval' and the tendency for an individual to answer either 'yes' or 'no' – there are yea-sayers and nay-sayers.

So the Langner Scale was subjected to scrutiny by obtaining responses from 404 adults. The results showed that women did not see the items as being more socially desirable than did the men; need for approval did not differentiate between the men and the women; and the women were definitely more inclined to say 'no' than 'yes'. This latter rather surprising finding would lead one to think that the excess of women reporting psychiatric symptoms would be if anything, an underestimate. One factor to be borne in mind when assessing the results of Clancy and Gove is that all the interviewers were women. It is remarkable how seldom the sex of the interviewer is considered in research into sex differences. Particularly so when there is a considerable body of psychological research showing that the sex of the interviewer, experimenter, psychologist, or whatever else you like to call them, affects the results obtained.

Convincing evidence has yet to be produced showing that women are more likely to acknowledge psychiatric symptoms than men. The evidence, if anything, is to the contrary.

(d) *Women have more reasons for being psychologically disturbed*. In a sense, Wilsnack (1973) and others may be right in saying that many women adopt 'masculine' behaviour and attitudes because they feel inadequate as women. But where we part company with them is in the implied assumption that it is necessarily a good thing to feel a secure and adequate female and that any deviation from this is undesirable. Might it not be argued that some women feel inadequate as women because theirs is an inadequate way of living life? If so, then such women can be seen as seeking to develop their lives and personalities and so become aggressive in a Kellian sense (1955). That is, they actively elaborate their construct systems. But this active elaboration leads them to behave in a way that contravenes the female stereotype laws. It is in the perception of this contravention that trouble ensues.

One way of dealing with perceived personal deviance is to live with it, and tolerate the subsequent stresses and strains. Alternatively, one can pretend that there is no problem there – that all is well in the best of all possible worlds. As a result a woman may glory in her femininity, and convince herself by behaving in ultra-feminine ways. However, if this effort to conform fails to convince her, then something more extreme becomes necessary. For instance, she may become super-dependent, submissive, weepy, and feminine and, if all else fails, be seen as depressed enough to be admitted to hospital where she ceases to be a woman and becomes a depressed patient. On the other hand, she may not resort to overt depression, but instead show her need for help by becoming dependent on drugs or alcohol.

If we consider psychological difficulties as an individual's efforts to deal with the problems in life as he or she sees them, then the questions we pose for our research may lead to our obtaining more useful answers.

Women's views of women mental patients

In a paper 'Sex and mental illness' (1975), nicely subtitled 'the generosity of females', Farina and Hagelauer discuss their studies on how men and women perceive someone whom they know has been mentally ill. A female 'confederate' was interviewed by some female clerks who were going to work with her. Half were told she came from a mental hospital and half that she was an ordinary job seeker. With half the clerks the 'confederate' behaved in a calm way and with the other half in a 'tense and nervous fashion'. The results were clear-cut. The mental history made no difference; it was the nervous behaviour that led to her being rejected.

When a similar experiment was carried out with a male 'confederate' and male interviewers, both the mental history and the behaviour led to him being rejected. Thinking it might be the setting that had influenced the first results with the women, the whole procedure was carried out again, this time in a Veterans' Administration Hospital. The results were the same – the women accepted the history but not the behaviour.

Farina and Hagelauer then set out to see if a male 'applicant' was as generously perceived by female interviewers as was the female 'confederate'. The results were as before. Women seem to be well-disposed towards someone who has been in a mental hospital, whereas men are not, but both are influenced by behaviour. She thinks these findings are unusual in that most research suggests that both men and women are suspicious of someone who has been in a mental hospital. She suggests that perhaps women are more influenced by the behaviour of the person with whom they are interacting while men take more notice of the history.

Therapy and the female sufferer

In this book *Sexual Identity Conflict* (1974), Green deals with the most radical treatment for dissatisfaction with one's sex-role – the sex change operation. It is strange after so much discussion about the unsatisfactory state of affairs in which women find themselves, to be told that, for every woman who wants to become a man, there are three to six men wanting to become women.

Green suggests four reasons for this suprising turn of events. First, there is a likelihood of more errors in the psychosexual development of men. Second, there is greater latitude allowed women with respect to cross-gender behaviour. Third, the first person a child identifies with is the mother, and it is only the boy who has a subsequent shift of identity. Fourth, it is more difficult to make a woman into a man. Green reports one surgeon as saying, 'It's easier to make a hole than a pole' (Green 1974: 102). Of passing interest is the fact that his own book *Sexual Identity Conflict* consist of 140 pages devoted to feminine boys and four pages to masculine girls.

But for most women the answer, if not drugs, is psychotherapy. For, not only are there more women than men in psychiatric hospitals, but of those having psychotherapy, more than two-thirds are women (Barrett *et al.* 1974). Since Broverman

(1972) and her colleagues have evidence suggesting that both male and female clinicians share the 'powerful negative assessment' of women, the women seeking treatment have to learn a difficult lesson – how to be a healthy adult as well as a healthy woman. It is hard work. Women tend to be given psychotherapy for twice as long as men (Fabrikant 1974). Fabrikant concludes that '... females in therapy are victimized by a social structure and therapeutic philosophy which keeps them dependent for as long as possible' (Fabrikant 1974:96).

Enquiring into reasons for seeking psychotherapy, Fabrikant reported that many women suffer from dissatisfaction either with the role of wife and mother, or from a conflict between this role and the strong desire for her own style of life. He also found that male therapists and male patients both thought that the majority of women could be fulfilled by being a wife and mother – but female therapists and female patients disagreed. This highlights the bind the women are in. It is possible that therapy will not provide the answer women seek, since 67 per cent of the women in Fabrikant's study had male therapists. It is doubtful if these figures differ markedly elsewhere in the Western world.

The American Psychological Association set up a task force to investigate sex bias, and their report was published in 1975. Concern is expressed about findings such as Broverman's. The task force think women in therapy may not be understood and may have foreign values imposed on them. For instance, women may have problems of which the therapists are unaware. A woman can be struggling with her fear of success and the male or female therapist be quite unaware that this can be a problem. There is also the whole problem of what are interpreted as appropriate behaviours for men and women. A woman may be construed as behaving in a 'masculine' way when verbally aggressive. But the implications of this behaviour are not necessarily that she is trying to castrate men, but simply that she has not developed the social skill of being self-assertive in a non-aggressive way.

There are many papers now on 'feminist' therapies (for example, Kirsch 1974; Barrett et al. 1974; Lerman 1974). The task force comments on Lerman's paper in which she characterizes the feminist form of therapy as distinctly non-authoritarian and which does not acknowledge the therapist as the authority figure. Lerman's woman patient needs to learn to distinguish between her own personal problems and the problems of the society in which she lives; to learn what behaviours are appropriate for her and what for society; to learn that self-interest is not necessarily bad and that guilt is not the necessary result of feeling dislike for her children or for the confining life that she leads.

Lerman's paper is entitled 'Feminist therapy? In search of a theory'. We could suggest she looks at personal construct theory. In its application to therapy, one of the guidelines governing the psychotherapeutic relationship is that the patient must be made aware that the therapist does not have the answers, nor does he think he has. The patient has the answers and, with the therapist in the search with her, they may both find an alternative way of looking at her world and the people in it. In most cases, the problems are not in the people and events surrounding her, but in her own construing or interpretation of those events (see Kelly 1955; Fransella 1975). A woman can accept the social restrictions on her life without having to like them. But the problems do not have to remain 'out there'. What happens if we construe events, our own and other people's behaviour, as the product of out-moded stereotyped attitudes? Will we not now get up and do something to alter the situation. We are only at the mercy of events and people if we construe ourselves as such.

Schonbar's article (1972) on the relevance of group therapy for sex-role identification is an example of a technique that could help such reconstruing. She thinks that part of the problem is that men and women have been brought up to believe in sex-role stereotypes and often feel unable to conform to them.

'Some women are amazed to learn that some men see them as destructively powerful because they are women, while they themselves feel eternally helpless and victimized for the very same reason. Members of both sexes are astonished to discover how tenaciously they themselves cling to the stereotypes they so bitterly denounce. Moreover, group therapy

provides an opportunity for seeing that there are many ways of being a person.'
(Schonbar 1972:543)

If a man and a woman act as co-therapists, they can, on occasion, deliberately break the stereotype by adopting opposite roles. The therapists act as invalidators of the person's present construing. Construct theory as applied to therapy seems particularly appropriate here. It is a theory of how people go about the business of living and of making sense of themselves and of life's events. It has no content such as the complexes of Freudian theory. Thus the therapist has no content to impose, except his own personal views. Even here there is less of a problem than with most therapies. For the most important skill the therapist has to develop is the ability to see life through the eyes of the other person. This is where real understanding lies. It does not mean accepting the world and its problems in the way the other person does. For the other person's view of the world is, of necessity, filtered through the therapist's own construct system and through the theoretical constructs he has about how construct systems operate. Therapy goes beyond understanding. Its aim is to help the individual to find alternative ways of seeing life and thus alternative ways of behaving. Kelly put it like this:

'... the task of pschotherapy is to get the human process going again so that life may go on and from where psychotherapy left off. There is no particular kind of interaction that is in itself a psychotherapeutic panacea, nor is there any particular set of techniques that are the techniques of choice for the personal construct theorist. The relationships between therapist and client and the techniques they employ may be as varied as the whole human repertory of relationships and techniques. It is the orchestration of techniques and the utilization of relationships in the on-going process of living and profiting from experience that makes psychotherapy a contribution to human life.'
(Kelly 1969:233)

ELEVEN

Maintenance and resistance to change of sex stereotypes

We accept that sex stereotypes exist, both in terms of roles and personality characteristics. We accept that many women fit uneasily within their confines, if not actively rebel against them. It therefore seems reasonable to ask 'why do they not give them up?' We have tried to demonstrate many of the reasons for their maintenance throughout this book. But two additional ways in which society is actively involved in sustaining the *status quo* is through mass media and literature, and particularly children's literature.

Maintenance

One possible starting point is with the public purveyors of stereotypes. In Chapter 4 we discussed the influence of parents on how children construe themselves and others. One of the activities of parents is to read a book at bed-time, and so the content of such books is presumably also influential. One study has been carried out by Jacklin and Mischel (1973) on stories for first to third grade children in North America and another by Maon (1974) on the content of textbooks for Israeli children.

Jacklin and Mischel in an article nicely entitled, 'As the twig is bent', analysed 270 stories. To start with, males were favoured at a purely numerical level.

	males	females
children	324	241
adults	256	124
total	580	365

These boys and girls behaved in typically stereotyped ways. Boys were more aggressive and indulged more in physical exertion and the solving of problems. While the girls were more often portrayed as being absorbed in fantasy, as using directing or demonstrating behaviour, and making both positive and negative statements about themselves. For instance, they would say such things as 'I have blue eyes' or 'I'm too stupid' much more than the boys would.

When adult, the men in the stories behaved as they had as boys, indulging in more problem solving behaviour and physical exertion, but aggression was reduced and instead of this they constructed and produced things. The women were shown as significantly more conformist and indulged in more general talk.

The environments in which the characters moved were then analysed. There were no sex differences for the children. However, with the adults, there were sex differences: men were more often to be found out of doors and in business, and the women in the home and in schools.

After an analysis of behaviour, environment, and the number of characters, came an analysis of the types of consequences resulting from actions. These were scored positive and negative and subdivided into consequences from: (1) others, for example praise, support; (2) self, for example self-praise, satisfaction; (3) the situation, for example reaching a goal; (4) chance, or the author's statements or the text.

For the child characters, rewards for boys came significantly

196

more often from their own actions and rewards for girls from situations. But as adults, males were shown as receiving their rewards from other people and as castigating themselves significantly more than women. The women only differed from girls in receiving significantly more neutral consequences, that is, the consequences could not be scored as either positive or negative results. As both the authors of this paper are women, it would be interesting to know whether men would have scored these consequences in a less neutral way.

There was also a significant change in the characters as we move from first grade to third grade books. First, female children become fewer and male adults increase. There are also increasing differences between the sexes and age groups in behaviour, environment in which the characters move, and in type of consequences. Jacklin and Mischel (1973) state that the stereotypic portrayal of male and female roles (both child and adult) increased with the grade level studied. They conclude that:

'Sex role stereotyping is pervasive in elementary readers. Girls and women appear less frequently and engage in distinctly different activities than boys and men. Females are rarely main characters in the stories: they seldom solve problems or do interesting things. Girls are depicted as fantasizing and talking about themselves. Women are shown as conforming and talking a great deal, though not about themselves. Men, on the other hand, construct and produce things, solve problems, and engage in various kinds of hard work and play.'   (Jacklin and Mischel 1973:85)

In the analysis of textbooks for nine-year-old Israeli children, Maon (1974) found just such clear-cut dichotomies between male and female characters.

Jacklin and Mischel refer to a study by Kirchner and Vondracek (1973) in which it was found that girls between the ages of three and six had come to realize that certain adult positions were not open to them. Conversely, boys perceive that more jobs will be available to them than to girls (Looft 1971). Since it seems unlikely that these children will have learned all about jobs and adult roles from observations within the family, the power of the written word, be it school books, comics, or traditional children's stories, must be given serious consideration as an early influence on the development of stereotyped sex attitudes. But they are also, of course, subjected to advertising.

Children's books clearly help present the sex-role stereotype to the child – the great, strong, aggressive, go-getter of a man and the submissive, charming, mother, housewife, whose horizon is no further than the kitchen sink. This is nicely demonstrated by the fact that advertisements often show the man as having his eyes on some distant horizon and the woman either gazing at her man or with eyes gently lowered. But although there must be a great deal of important information tucked away in the archives of advertisers about how women react to advertisements and what they think about them, there is hardly any information readily available.

In her article, 'The image of woman in advertising', Komisar (1971) describes how a group of women demonstrated outside Macey's store in New York City in December 1969, against the advertising campaign of Mattel Toys. She comments that *Life* magazine had a Mattel advertisement with sentiments such as, 'Because girls dream about being a ballerina, Mattel makes Dancerina ... a pink confection in a silken blouse and ruffled tutu ...' 'Because boys were born to build and learn, Mattel, makes Tog'l (a set of building blocks for creative play).' This was apparently followed by an illustration of a boy playing with

'... imaginative and fantastic creatures that challenge young minds to think as they build ... Because boys are curious about things big and small, Mattel makes Super-Eyes, a telescope that boys can have in one ingenious set of optically engineered lenses and scopes ...'

(Komisar 1971 : 305)

A wealth of data may be expected to exist among market research reports. Market researchers spend a great deal of time asking people what they think about products. There are several examples that we could give, but much work is based on 'two-steps removed' factor analytic-type of data rather than on more direct questioning of women. However, that does not mean we cannot learn something about women – mainly the 'housewife' – from such studies as we can from the few that are of a more direct nature.

One example is that of Greeno, Sommers, and Kernan (1973). One hundred and ninety housewives, aged between thirty and forty-five, with at least one child, living in single, detached houses in Texas, were asked to sort out thirty-eight products. These women were described as being 'thoroughly involved with obtaining, using, and developing aspirations for consumer products and tend to be excellent culture bearers' (Greeno, Sommers, and Kernan 1973:64). The actual question asked was not specified, but the housewives had to rank the thirty-eight items on the basis of some personal preference – perhaps which product they liked the most. They also filled out a personality questionnaire which gave scores for 'ascendancy', 'responsibility', 'emotional stability', and 'sociability'.

These answers were then statistically analysed to produce clusters of items. The main cluster consisted of: stove, refrigerator, washer, bread, iron, shortening, flour, potatoes, dresses, hand-soap, toothpaste, and TV set. The authors named this cluster *homemakers*. By relating this to the other data obtained from women who put these items high on the list, the authors were able to say that the homemakers could be described as

'representing the traditional kitchen-bound housewife. Comparatively speaking, these women are low on ascendancy, high on responsibility, moderately stable, and not very sociable ... more white than black, of comparatively modest means, and decidedly working-class ... This housewife's daily fare likely consists of "doing the best she can" for her family on limited means.'

(Greeno, Sommers, and Kernan 1973:68)

The other clusters were described as *matriarchs, variety girls, cinderellas, glamour girls, and media-conscious glamour girls*.

From more direct methods we get another type of information. For example, thirty men and women were interviewed to find out their attitudes to teeth. For women to lose teeth is apparently worse than to lose hair, whereas for men the opposite is the case. The women also saw a double standard operating. The men were seen as being willing to put up with aspects of appearance that they would never put up with in a woman. That is, women's teeth have to be cleaner and more shiny, their breath sweeter, and their hair sleeker and better groomed.

In another (also unpublished) study, designed to investigate the attitudes of men and women to advertising in general rather than specific advertisements, there emerged a stereotype of those who were influenced by a lot of advertising. These gullible people are unintelligent, unsophisticated, uncritical, immature, and – but of course – female. As with the sex-role stereotype, so here, both men and women agree in seeing women as gullible (see Bem 1974).

Where does change come from?

We could go on giving interesting and provocative examples of such research. But all that is happening is that one is being fed back the sex stereotype in its most extreme form. The evidence adds up to the conclusion that women have, by and large, 'bought' the stereotype of themselves and all that product merchandizing does is to help ensure that it does not change. We might therefore conclude that change must start with children's books and advertising. Let the writers and the designers stop being sexist and give us books and advertisements about individual people. But, if they did this, they would not sell their books or their products and would soon go out of business. Others would then take their place and so on. Clearly these are not the people to whom we should be looking to lead the change.

Perhaps our starting point should be individual men and women. That seems simple enough. Supposing we focus on women. A common complaint is that if only women would get their ideas sorted out, they and everyone else would be much happier. So why are they finding it so difficult?

Here is the case of one woman who really is concerned about women and their place in society. She joined a 'consciousness-raising' group and found it a painful process. It is one thing to come to the conclusion that one's behaviour or attitude is in fact submissive, dependent and generally conformist. But then the question posed is, what does one do about it? What are the alternative ways of behaving that are open to women? She might decide that being submissive is really not 'her', but something she has learned in response to social pressures. But who can help her find out what alternative ways there are of behaving in those situations in which she is used to behaving submissively? There are various behaviours that are traditionally male, but she does not want to be construed as masculine either.

The answer seems to be that there is no answer. Any change a woman manages to produce in herself will still be subject to the stereotypical constraints of her society. One of the jobs of the psychotherapist is to help the patient work out for herself alternative ways of behaving. In Kelly's view (1970), all behaviour is an experiment. Behaviour is a way in which we test out our views of ourselves and society. So what if she goes and behaves in an assertive way and asks the behavioural question, 'when I am assertive, will this man react to me more as an individual than as just a good, submissive woman?' The odds are she will be construed by the man as being deviant to the general stereotype and, according to his personal view of life, he will either see her as castrating him, as simply neurotic, or as one of those feminist bitches; 'Oh God, when will they give it all up and go home where they were meant to be and where they are obviously happiest!'

There must be an interplay between our behavioural questions and the answers we get. And the answers in turn will influence our view of ourselves and the future behavioural questions we ask. So it is no good simply trying to break away from one's own stereotype. One has to have somewhere to go. One has to have some idea of what alternatives are open to oneself, as a woman who wishes to become a person; and it is not easy to find out what that person is. One would have to look for something that is neither particularly masculine nor feminine, but perhaps a kind of universal androgyny, which is unlikely to be successful unless men are also willing to change.

However, men (and many women) resist change. And the reason why is one of the most important questions to which an answer must be found. One suggestion stems from Kelly's notion of threat (Kelly 1955). Let us suppose that men, in general, are prepared to change. They see the need to change. Let us also suppose that being male, or masculine, is a central construct in their system. To be masculine implies all those things that are most dear to the man's heart. This realization of the need to change will produce a massive threat. This, in construct theory terms, is *the awareness of imminent comprehensive change in one's core structures*. For a man to contemplate that he might actually come to construe women as individuals and not as belonging to that great group of 'the opposite sex' might mean he would have to give up his own 'male' stereotype view of himself and prove to himself, personally, that he is strong, virile, capable, well-balanced, and all else that makes him the man he is.

One way of dealing with threat is to show hostility. This is the *continued effort to extort validational evidence in favour of a type of social prediction which has already been recognized as a failure*. A man may agree that women are having a raw deal and that things must change. But, having contemplated the massive nature of the change, he is not personally able to carry it through. So he has to provide evidence for himself that his original way of construing was really the right one all along. Women are women and that is all there is to it. He just had a bad dream in which women suddenly ceased to be a background against which he could constantly seek confirmation that he is a man. Thus he seeks to involve women he knows are interested in the feminist movement, in long discussions, saying deliberately provocative things. When they become annoyed and answer back in similarly provocative terms, he can dismiss them and convince himself that all that happens to women when they try to change things is that they behave unlike women.

Threat will also make some women behave in hostile ways. Those who have spent their lives living the part, putting up with erring husbands for the sake of the children, putting up with the children for her own sake, are not going to take kindly to being made aware that there really was an alternative.

But of course changes in society do take place over the years, or perhaps overnight if accompanied by blood. The feminist movement is helping men to think of women in a way that they have never been forced to before. But, if there seems a chance that they might succeed, or that things might move too fast, there will be a hardening of the categories. An exhibition of hostility, perhaps outwardly as well as in the Kellian sense (1955), will occur. It is important that this is dealt with sympathetically. The sting must be taken out of the tail of the threat.

Changing relationships and changing institutions

If changing personal relationships were all that were needed to change sex-role stereotypes, the task would be difficult enough. But there is more to it than this. For our social institutions are built on the assumption that women are and should be restricted to particular roles. We see this assumption as a myth in many ways, true neither of the past nor of the present. Nonetheless, the way we organize working life and family life at present, forces most women into one mould. As a result, it constantly feeds back to women one particular image of themselves, and makes it very difficult to develop new images.

Consider, for example, a mother of two children who also has to work. She probably lives within reach of her husband's job, so she is limited to whatever is available in the area. She can only have a job if there is someone to mind the children, and if it fits in with nursery or school hours. Even if she has training, which many women do not, there is probably little choice of job. It is likely to be boring and badly-paid, with little chance of promotion. She can hardly do overtime or go to Union meetings. She cannot take on a position which needs commitment, or allows her much independence and responsibility. How is she to find out that she has these qualities? Or that she might enjoy her work? (And, incidentally, how is her husband to find out that he enjoys looking after children?)

In Chapter 7 we described how some women set about making new roles for themselves within their families. Not surprisingly they aimed for the kinds of readjustments that can be made without major changes in society. If you have the money, it is easier to pay a home-help than to get your husband to do some housework. It may sometimes (by no means always!) be easier to persuade a husband to do some housework than to get the State to provide nursery schools, or an employer to provide flexible working hours. If you have neither money nor a willing husband, it is harder. These experiments in role-making are courageous and important, but they are not enough to change how women see themselves.

It is not the purpose of this book to detail the practical problems which women face, nor to provide a blue-print (even if we had one) of the future. But we can speculate on some of the possible kinds of changes that might have to be made to allow women to have a different view of themselves.

If, for instance, we decide that women should be free both to be mothers and to work, with the same opportunities as men, then working life would have to be reorganized. Apart from doing away with outright discrimination, it would be necessary to adapt working hours to suit people who are looking after children, to make part-time work more available, and to change career structures so that people who take time out to have children can return to work. It would also be necessary to provide good crêches and nurseries for everyone who needs them. If we decide that men should do as much housework as women, or have the freedom to be equally involved in bringing up children – the chance to be real fathers – then their jobs and working lives would have to be reorganized in the same way. If we decide that all women and men who wish to should be able to devote themselves solely to looking after their small children, then they would have to be paid enough so as not to be forced to work. Why not? After all, bringing up children is a very important job and serves the whole of society.

Not everyone would want these particular changes. We are not advocating them for everyone.

Inevitably the problems and priorities are different for people in different situations. Highly educated women face conflicts which may be peculiar to them at the moment. They are pressured on the one hand to use their abilities and training and to 'fulfil' themselves at work; and on the other to put being wives and mothers first. At the same time they have and can see more real alternatives than most people of either sex.

This may be one reason why they are more actively seeking the freedom to work.

The dilemmas facing working women differ in a number of ways. Many work from necessity not choice; their work is exploitation, not fulfilment; yet it also makes motherhood more difficult. Others who would like the money, independence, and social contacts that work can bring, are confined to the house with their children.

To make such changes possible, would require a major social reorganization. This sort of change is not brought about simply by persuasion and rational argument. The strategies are not the same as in changing personal relationships, for real conflicts of interest and power are involved. If the majority of women workers are to be more than cheap exploited labour, employers have to pay them higher wages – someone has to pay for nursery schools ... and so on. To achieve these conditions women have to be able to demand their rights – an activity at which women are encouraged to be bad. Moreover, it cannot be done by individuals on their own.

Only if we move away from our stereotypes, can we change the world outside. And only in the process of changing the world outside can we begin to create new ways of seeing ourselves. The two cannot happen separately. Despite all the research, each woman has to discover herself for herself – individually and together with others.

References

ADAM, R. (1975) *A Woman's Place 1910–1975*. London: Chatto & Windus.

ALMQUIST, E. and ANGRIST, S. (1970) Career Salience and A typicality of Occupational Choice among College Women. *Journal of Marriage and the Family* 32:242–9.

AMERICAN PSYCHOLOGICAL ASSOCIATION (1975) Sex Bias and Sex-Role Stereotyping in Psychotherapeutic Practice. Report. *American Psychologist* 30:1169–75.

ANGRIST, S. (1972) Variations in Women's Adult Aspirations during College. *Journal of Marriage and the Family* 34:465–8.

AUSUBEL, D. P., BALTHAZAR, E., ROSENTHAL, I., BLACKMAN, L. S., SCHPOONT, S. H., and WELKOWITZ, J. (1954) Perceived Parent Attitudes and Determinants of Children's Ego Structure. *Child Development* 25:173–83.

BAHR, S. (1974) Effects on Power and Division of Labor in the Family. In L. W. Hoffman and F. I. Nye (eds.), *Working Mothers*. London: Jossey-Bass.

BAILYN, L. (1964) Notes on the Role of Choice in the Psychology of Women. *Daedalus* 93:700–10.

BANNER, L. (1974) *Women in Modern America: A Brief History.* New York: Harcourt Brace Jovanovich.

BANNISTER, D. (1977) The Child's Construing of Self. In, *Nebraska Symposium on Motivation 1976.* Lincoln: Nebraska University Press.

BARDWICK, J. (1971) *Psychology of Women.* New York: Harper & Row.

BARRETT, C., BERG, P., EATON, E., and POMEROY, L. (1974) Implications of Women's Liberation and the Future of Psychotherapy. *Psychotherapy: Theory, Research and Practice* 11:11–15.

BARRY, H., BACON, M., and CHILD, I. (1957) A Cross-Cultural Survey of Some Sex Differences in Socialization. *Journal of Abnormal and Social Psychology* 55:327–32.

BART, P. (1968) Social Structure and Vocabularies of Discomfort: what happened to female hysteria? *Journal of Health and Social Behaviour* 9:188–93.

—— (1969) Why Women's Status Changes in Middle-Age: the turns of the social ferris wheel. *Sociological Symposium* 3:1–18.

—— (1971) Depression in Middle-Aged Women. In V. Gornick and B. Moran (eds.), *Woman in Sexist Society.* New York: Basic Books.

BEM, D. and BEM, S. (1970) Case-Study of a Non-Conscious Ideology: training the woman to know her place. In D. Bem (ed.), *Beliefs, Attitudes and Human Affairs.* Belmont, California: Brooks Cole.

BEM, S. (1974) The Measurement of Psychological Androgyny. *Journal of Consulting and Clinical Psychology* 42:155–62.

—— (1975) Personal Communication. Cited in E. Maccoby and C. Jacklin (eds.), *The Psychology of Sex Difference.* London: Oxford University Press.

BENDO, A. and FELDMAN, H. (1973) A Comparison of the Self-Concept of Low-Income Women with and without Husbands Present. *Cornell Journal of Social Relations* 9:53–85.

BENNETT, E. and COHEN, L. (1959) Men and Women: Personality Patterns and Contrasts. *Genetic Psychology Monographs* 59:101–55.

BERGER, B., HACKETT, B., and MILLAR, R. (1972) Child-Rearing Practices in the Communal Family. In H. P. Dreitzel (ed.), Family, Marriage and the Struggle of the Sexes. London: Collier–Macmillan.

BERNARD, J. (1966) *Academic Women.* Cleveland, Ohio: World.
—— (1973) *The Future of Marriage.* New York: Bantam Books.
—— (1976) Maternal Deprivation: a new twist. *Contemporary Psychology* 21:172–3.

BERNSTEIN, B. (1971) *Class, Codes and Control: Volume 1 Theoretical Studies Towards a Sociology of Language.* London: Routledge & Kegan Paul.

BIDDLE, B. and THOMAS, E. (eds.) (1966) *Role Theory: Concepts and Research.* New York: Wiley.

BILLER, H. (1973) Sex-Role Uncertainty and Psychopathology. *Journal of Individual Psychology* 29:24–5.

BLOMQUIST, K. (1962) An Investigation of Attitudes towards Advancement. Cited in H. Holter (1970) *Sex Roles and Social Structure.* Oslo: Universitetsforlaget.

BOTT, E. (1957) *Family and Social Network.* London: Tavistock Publications.

BRADBURN, N. and CAPLOVITZ, D. (1965) *Reports on Happiness: a pilot study of behaviour related to mental health.* Chicago: Aldine.

BRADY, J. and LEVITT, E. (1965) The Scalability of Sexual Experiences. *Psychological Record* 15:275–9.

BRANDT, R. (1958) The Accuracy of Self Estimate: a Measure of Self-Concept Reality. *Genetic Psychology Monographs* 58:55–99.

BREEN, D. (1975) *The Birth of a First Child: Towards an understanding of Femininity.* London: Tavistock Publications.

BRONFENBRENNER, U. (1970) *Two Worlds of Childhood.* London: George Allen & Unwin.

BROVERMAN, I., BROVERMAN, D., CLARKSON, F., ROSEN-KRANTZ, P., and VOGEL, S. (1970) Sex-Role Stereotype and Clinical Judgements of Mental Health. *Journal of Consulting and Clinical Psychology* 34:1–7.

BROVERMAN, I., VOGEL, S., BROVERMAN, D., CLARKSON, F.,

and ROSENKRANTZ, P. (1972) Sex-Role Stereotypes: a current appraisal. *Journal of Social Issues* 28:59–78.

BROWN, G., BHROLCHAIN, M., and HARRIS, T. (1975) Social Class and Psychiatric Disturbance among Women in an Urban Population. *Sociology* 9:225–54.

BRUN-GULBRANSDEN, S. (1958) Kjønnsrolle og Asosialitet. Cited in H. Holter (1970) *Sex Roles and Social Structure*. Oslo: Universitetsforlaget.

BUMPASS, L. and WESTOFF, C. (1970) The Perfect Contraceptive Population. *Science* 169:1177.

BURGESS, E. and WALLIN, P. (1953) *Engagement and Marriage*. Philadelphia: J. P. Lippincott.

BUSFIELD, J. (1974) Ideologies and Reproduction. In M. Richards (ed.), *The Integration of a Child into a Social World*. Cambridge: Cambridge University Press.

CARLSON, R. (1965) Stability and Change in the Adolescent's Self-Image. *Child Psychology* 36:659–66.

—— (1970) On the Structure of Self-Esteem: comments on Ziller's formulation. *Journal of Consulting and Clinical Psychology* 34:264–8.

—— (1971) Sex Differences in Ego Functioning: exploratory studies of agency and communion. *Journal of Consulting and Clinical Psychology* 37:267–77.

CARLSON, R. and LEVY, N. (1968) Brief Method for Assessing Social-Personal Orientation. *Psychological Reports* 23:911–14.

—— —— (1970) Self, Values and Affects: derivations from Tomkins' polarity theory. *Journal of Personality and Social Psychology* 16:338–45.

CHESLER, P. (1972) *Women and Madness*. New York: Avon Books.

CHETWYND, J., STEWART, R., and POWELL, G. (1974) Social Attitudes towards the Obese Physique. Paper read at 10th European Conference on Psychosomatic Research, Edinburgh.

CHODOROW, N. (1971) Being and Doing: A Cross-Cultural Examination of the Socialisation of Males and Females. In V. Gornick and B. K. Moran (eds.), *Woman in Sexist Society*. London: New English Library.

—— (1974) Family Structure and Feminine Personality. In

209

M. Z. Rosaldo and L. Lamphere (eds.), *Woman, Culture and Society*. Stanford, California: Stanford University Press.

CHOMBART DE LAUWE, P. (1962) The Status of Women in French Urban Society. *International Social Science Journal* 14:26–65.

CLANCY, K. and GOVE, W. (1974) Sex Differences in Mental Illness: an analysis of response bias in self-reports. *American Journal of Sociology* 80:205–16.

CLARKSON, F., VOGEL, S., BROVERMAN, I., BROVERMAN, D., and ROSENKRANTZ, P. (1970) Family Size and Sex-Role Stereotypes. *Science* 167:390–2.

CLAUTOUR, S. and MOORE, T. (1969) Attitudes of Twelve-Year-Old Children to Present and Future Life Roles. *Human Development* 12:221–38.

COBLINER, W. G. (1970) Teen-age Out-of-Wedlock Pregnancy. *Bulletin of the New York Academy of Medicine* 46:438–47.

COHEN, M. (1966) Personal Identity and Sexual Identity. *Psychiatry* 29:1–14.

COLEMAN, J. (1961) *The Adolescent Society*. Glencoe: Free Press.

CONSTANTINOPLE, A. (1973) Masculinity–Femininity: an exception to a famous dictum. *Psychological Bulletin* 80: 389–407.

COOKE, W. (1943) *Essentials of Gynaecology*. Philadelphia: J. P. Lippincott.

COOPERSMITH, S. (1967) *The Antecedents of Self-Esteem*. San Francisco: W. H. Freeman.

CRANDELL, V. (1963) Achievement. In H. W. Stevenson (ed.), *Child Psychology: Sixty-second Yearbook of the National Society for the Study of Education*. Chicago: University of Chicago Press.

CRISP, A. (1970) Premorbid Factors in Adult Disorders of Weight, with Particular Reference to Primary Anorexia Nervosa (weight phobia): a literature review. *Journal of Psychosomatic Research* 14:1–22.

CULLEN, J. (1972) Nurseries. In M. Wandor *The Body Politic*. London: Stage 1.

D'AUGELLI, J. and CROSS, H. (1975) Relationship of Sex Guilt and Moral Reasoning to Premarital Sex in College Women and in Couples. *Journal of Consulting and Clinical Psychology* 43:40–7.

DAVIDSON, H. and LANG, G. (1960) Children's Perceptions of their Teachers' Feelings towards them Related to Self-Perception, School Achievement and Behaviour. *Journal of Experimental Education* 29:107–18.

DE MARTINO, M. (1969) *The New Female Sexuality*. New York: Julian.

DEPARTMENT OF HEALTH AND SOCIAL SECURITY (1972) *Health and Personal Social Services Statistics for England and Wales*. London: HMSO.

DEVERSON, J. and LINDSAY, K. (1975) *Voices From the Middle Class*. London: Hutchinson.

DIDERICHSEN, B., PETERSON, K., RØSTBOL, B., and SANDAHL, K. (1975) Kønsrolleopfattelse og Miljø. *Nordisk Psykologi* 27:86–98.

DOUVAN, E. (1963) Employment and the Adolescent. In F. I. Nye and L. W. Hoffman (eds.), *The Employed Mother in America*. Chicago: Rand McNally.

DOUVAN, E. and ADELSON, J. (1966) *The Adolescent Experience*. New York: Wiley.

DRAEGER, H. (1972) The Job Market and Women. *New York Post* October 27:20.

EHRMANN, W. (1959) *Premarital Dating Behaviour*. New York: Holt, Rinehart and Winston.

ELMAN, J., PRESS, A., and ROSENKRANTZ, P. (1970) Sex-Roles and Self-Concepts: real and ideal. *Journal of Social Issues* 28:59–78.

EMPEY, L. T. (1958) Role Expectations of Young Women Regarding Marriage and a Career. *Journal of Marriage and Family Living* 20:152–5.

EPSTEIN, C. (1970) *Woman's Place*. Berkeley: University of California Press.

EPSTEIN, G. and BRONZAFT, A. (1972) Female Freshmen View their Roles as Women. *Journal of Marriage and the Family* 34:671–2.

FABRIKANT, B. (1974) The Psychotherapist and the Female Patient: perceptions and change. In V. Franks and V. Burtle (eds.), *Women in Therapy*. New York: Brunner/Mazel.

FARINA, A. and HAGELAUER, H. (1975) Sex and Mental Illness : the generosity of females. *Journal of Consulting and Clinical Psychology* 43 : 122.

FARLEY, J. (1974) Co-education and College Women. *Cornell Journal of Relations* 9 : 87–97.

FARMER, H. and BOHN, M. (1970) Home-Career Conflict Reduction and the Level of Career Interest in Women. *Journal of Counseling Psychology* 17 : 228 32.

FEATHER, N. and RAPHELSON, A. (1974) Fear of Success in Australian and American Student Groups : motive or sex-role stereotype? *Journay of Personality* 42 : 190–201.

FELDMAN, M. and FELDMAN, H. (1973) The Low-Income Liberated Woman. *Human Ecology Forum* 4 : 13–16.

FERNBERGER, S. (1948) Persistence of Stereotypes Concerning Sex Differences. *Journal of Abnormal and Social Psychology* 43 : 97–101.

FOGARTY, M., RAPOPORT, R., and RAPOPORT, R. N. (1971) *Sex, Career and Family.* London : P. E. P. and George Allen & Unwin.

FRANCK, K. and ROSEN, E. (1948) Projective Test of Masculinity–Femininity. *Journal of Consulting Psychology* 13 : 247–56.

FRANSELLA, F. (1972) *Personal Change and Reconstruction.* London : Academic Press.

—— (1975) *Need to Change?* 'Essential Psychology' Series, P. Herriot (ed.). London : Methuen.

—— (1977) The Self and the Stereotype. In D. Bannister (ed.), *New Perspectives in Personal Construct Theory.* London : Academic Press.

FRANSELLA, F. and BANNISTER, D. (1977) *Repertory Grid Technique.* London : Academic Press.

FRANSELLA, F. and CRISP, A. (1974) Comparisons of Weight Concepts in a Group of (1) Neurotic, (2) 'Normal' and (3) Anorexic Females. Paper read at 10th European Conference on Psychosomatic Research, Edinburgh.

FRENCH, E. and LESSER, G. (1964) Some Characteristics of the Achievement Motive in Women. *Journal of Abnormal and Social Psychology* 68 : 119–28.

FREUD, S. (1962) Creative Writers and Daydreaming. In

J. Strachey (ed.), *The Standard Edition of the Complete Psychological Works of Sigmund Freud*. Vol. 9. London: Hogarth.

FRIDAY, N. (1975) *My Secret Garden*. New York: Virago.

FRIEDMAN, A. (1970) Hostility Factors and Clinical Improvement in Depressed Patients. *Archives of General Psychiatry* 23:524–37.

GARAI, J. and SCHEINFELD, A. (1968) Sex Differences in Mental and Behavioural Traits. *Genetic Psychology Monographs* 77: 169–229.

GAVRON, H. (1975) *The Captive Wife*. London: Penguin Books.

GILL, L. and SPILKA, B. (1962) Some Non-Intellectual Correlates of Academic Achievement among Mexican–American Secondary School Students. *Journal of Educational Psychology* 53:144–9.

GOLDBERG, P. (1968) Are Women Prejudiced against Women? *Trans-action* 5:28–30.

GOLDBERG, S. and LEWIS, M. (1969) Play Behaviour in the Year-Old Infant: early sex differences. *Child Development* 40:21–31.

GOLLIN, G. (1972) Family Surrogates in Colonial America: the Moravian experiment. In M. Gordon (ed.), *The Nuclear Family in Crisis: The Search for an Alternative*. London: Harper.

GOODE, W. J. (1960) A Theory of Role Strain. *American Sociological Review* 25:483–96.

GORDON, F. and HALL, D. (1974) Self-Image and Stereotypes of Femininity: their Relationship to Women's Role Conflicts and Coping. *Journal of Applied Psychology* 59:241–3.

GORDON, M. (ed.) (1972) *The Nuclear Family in Crisis: The Search for an Alternative*. London: Harper & Row.

GORNICK, V. and MORAN, B. (1971) *Women in Sexist Society*. New York: Basic Books.

GOVE, W. and TUDOR, J. (1973) Adult Sex Roles and Mental Illness. *American Journal of Sociology* 78:812–35.

GREEN, E. (1974) *Sexual Identity Conflict*. New York: Duckworth.

GREENO, D., SOMMERS, M., and KERNAN, J. (1973) Personality and Implicit Behaviour Patterns. *Journal of Marketing Research* 10:63–9.

GRIMM, E. (1969) Women's Attitudes and Reactions to Childbearing. In G. D. Goldman and D. S. Milman (eds.), *Modern Woman*. Springfield, Illinois: Charles C. Thomas.

GRIMM, E. and VENET, W. (1966) The Relationship of Emotional Adjustment and Attitudes to the Course and Outcome of Pregnancy. *Psychosomatic Medicine* 28:34–48.

GUBER, S. (1969) Sex Role and the Feminine Personality. In G. D. Goldman and D. S. Milman (eds.), *Modern Woman*. Springfield, Illinois: Charles C. Thomas.

GUMP, J. (1972) Sex-Role Attitudes and Psychological Well-Being. *Journal of Social Issues* 28:79–92.

HAAVIO-MANNILA, E. (1972) Sex-Role Attitudes in Finland, 1966–70. *Journal of Social Issues* 28:93–110.

HALL, D. (1972) A Model for Coping with Role-Conflict: The role behaviour of college educated women. *Administrative Science Quarterly* 17:471–86.

HALL, D. and MOHR, G. (1933) Prenatal Attitudes of Primiparae. *Mental Hygiene* 17:226–34.

HALLER, M. and ROSENMAYR, L. (1971) The Pluridimensionality of Work Commitment. *Human Relations* 24:501–18.

HANFORD, J. (1968) Pregnancy as a State of Conflict. *Psychological Reports* 22:1313–42.

HARITON, B. and SINGER, J. (1974) Women's Fantasies during Sexual Intercourse: normatives and theoretical implications. *Journal of Consulting and Clinical Psychology* 42:313–22.

HARTLEY, R. E. (1960) Children's Concepts of Male and Female Róles. *Derrill–Palmer Quarterley* 6(3):153–63.

HARTNETT, O. (1975) The Role of Psychology in the Propagation of Female Stereotypes. In Jane Chetwynd (ed.), *Sex-Role Stereotyping & Occupational Psychology*. Proceedings Symposium of annual conference of the British Psychological Society, Nottingham.

HARTUP, W., MOORE, S., and SAGER, G. (1963) Avoidance of Inappropriate Sex-Typing by Young Children. *Journal of Consulting Psychology* 27:467–73.

HAUSER, S. and SHAPIRO, R. (1973) Differentiation of Adolescent Self-Images. *Archives of General Psychiatry* 29:63–8.

HAWLEY, P. (1971) What Women Think Men Think. *Journal of Counseling Psychology* 18:193–9.

HEIMAN, J. (1975) Lady's Relish. *Psychology Today*.

HELSON, R. (1961) Creativity, Sex and Mathematics. *Proceedings of the Conference on the Creative Person*. Institute for Personality Assessment and Research and University Extension, University of California, Berkeley.

—— (1972) The Changing Image of the Career Woman. *Journal of Social Issues* 28(2):33–46.

HERN, W. (1971) Is Pregnancy Really Normal? *Family Planning Perspectives* 3:5–10.

HEYMAN, D. (1970) Does a Wife Retire? *Gerontologist* 10:54–6.

HINKLE, D. (1965) *The Change of Personal Constructs from the Viewpoint of a Theory of Implications*. Unpublished Ph.d. thesis, Ohio State University.

HOBART, C. (1973) Egalitarianism after Marriage: an attitude study of French and English-speaking Canadians. In M. Stephenson (ed.), *Women in Canada*. Toronto: New Press.

HOFFMAN, L. (1963) The Decision to Work. In F. Nye and L. Hoffman (eds.), *The Employed Mother in America*. Chicago: Rand McNally.

—— (1972) Early Childhood Experiences and Women's Achievement Motives. *Journal of Social Issues* 28:129–55.

—— (1974a) Fear of Success in Males and Females: 1965 and 1971. *Journal of Consulting and Clinical Psychology* 42:353–8.

—— (1974b) Psychological Factors. In L. Hoffman and F. Nye (eds.), *Working Mothers*. San Francisco: Jossey–Bass.

HOFFMAN, L. and NYE, F. (eds.) (1974) *Working Mothers*. San Francisco: Jossey–Bass.

HOLLENDER, J. (1972) Sex Differences in Sources of Social Self-Esteem. *Journal of Consulting and Clinical Psychology* 38:343–7.

HOLTER, H. (1970) *Sex Roles and Social Structure*. Oslo: Universitetsforlaget.

HORNER, M. (1968) Sex Differences in Achievement Motivation and Performance in Competitive and Non-Competitive Situations. Unpublished Ph.d. dissertation, University of Michigan.

—— (1970) Femininity and Successful Achievement: a basic inconsistency. In J. Bardwick, E. Douvan, M. Horner, and D. Gutmann (eds.), *Feminine Personality and Conflict*. Belmont, California: Brooks–Cole.

—— (1972) Toward an Understanding of Achievement-Related

Conflicts in Women. *Journal of Social Issues* 28:157–75.

HOY, R. (1973) The Meaning of Alcoholism for Alcoholics: a repertory grid study. *British Journal of Social and Clinical Psychology* 12:98–9.

HUANG, L. (1971) Sex-Role Stereotypes and Self-Concepts among American and Chinese Students. *Journal of Comparative Family Studies* 2:215–34.

HUBERT, J. (1974) Belief and Reality: social factors in pregnancy and childbirth. In M. Richards (ed), *The Integration of a Child into a Social World*. Cambridge: Cambridge University Press.

HUMPHREY, M. (1969) *The Hostage Seekers: A Study of Childless and Adopting Couples*. London: Longmans.

—— (1975) Parenthood – Fate or Fulfilment? Proceedings of the annual conference of the British Psychological Society, University of York.

IZARD, C. and CAPLAN, S. (1974) Sex Differences in Emotional Responses to Erotic Literature. *Journal of Consulting and Clinical Psychology* 42:468.

JACKLIN, C. and MISCHEL, H. (1973) As the Twig is Bent: sex role stereotyping in early readers. *School Psychology Digest* 2:30–8.

JACOBS, B. (1972) The Crisis of the Unwanted Pregnancy. *Marriage Guidance* 14:17–20.

JACOBSON, L. and NILSSON, A. (1967) Post-partum Mental Disorder in an Unselected Sample: the influence of parity. *Journal of Psychosomatic Research* 10:317–25.

JANIS, I. (1971) *Stress and Frustration*. New York: Harcourt Brace Jovanovich.

JOURARD, S. and REMY, R. (1955) Perceived Parental Attitudes, the Self and Security. *Journal of Consulting Psychology* 19:364–6.

KAPLAN, H. (1973) Self-Derogation and Social Position: interaction effects of sex, race, education, and age. *Social Psychology* 8:92–9.

KELLY, G. (1955) *The Psychology of Personal Constructs*. New York: Norton.

—— (1969) The Psychotherapeutic Relationship. In B. Maher (ed.), *Clinical Psychology and Personality*. New York: Wiley.

—— (1970) Behaviour is an Experiment. In D. Bannister (ed.), *Perspectives in Personal Construct Theory*. London: Academic Press.

KESSEN, W. (ed.) (1975) *Childhood in China*. New Haven: Yale University Press.

KIMBALL, M. (1973) Women and Success: a basic conflict? In M. Stephenson (ed.), *Women in Canada*. Toronto: New Press.

KIRCHENER, R. and VONDRACEK, S. (1973) What Do You Want to Be When You Grow Up? Vocational Choice in Children Aged Three to Six. Paper presented at the Society for Research in Child Development.

KIRSCH, B. (1974) Consciousness-Raising Groups as Therapy for Women. In V. Franks and V. Burtle (eds.), *Women in Therapy*. New York: Brunner/Mazel.

KLACKENBERG-LARSSON, I. (1974) Bestiaire 4–8 Years. Compte-rendu de la XIIe Réunion, Centre International de l'Enfance, Paris.

KLEMMACK, D. and EDWARDS, J. (1973) Women's Acquisition of Stereotyped Occupational Aspirations. *Sociology and Social Research* 57:540–5.

KOGAN, W., BOE, E., and GOCKA, E. (1968) Personality Changes in Unwed Mothers Following Parturition. *Journal of Clinical Psychology* 24:3–11.

KOHLBERG, L. (1966) A Cognitive-Development Analysis of Children's Sex-role Concepts and Attitudes. In E. Maccoby (ed.), *The Development of Sex Differences*. Stanford, California: Stanford University Press.

KOMAROVSKY, M. (1946) Cultural Contradictions and Sex Roles. *American Journal of Sociology* 52:184–9.

—— (1967) *Blue Collar Marriage*. New York: Vintage Books.

KOMISAR, L. (1971) The Image of Women in Advertising. In V. Gornick and B. Moran (eds.), *Women in Sexist Society*. New York: Basic Books.

LANDAU, B. (1973) Women and Mental Illness. *Ontario Psychologist* 5:51–7.

LANGNER, T. (1962) A Twenty-two Item Screening Score of Psychiatric Symptoms Indicating Impairment. *Journal of Health and Human Behavior* 3:269–76.

LEIGHTON, D., LEIGHTON, A., HARDIN, J., MACKLIN, D., and

MacMILLAN, A. (1963) *The Character of Danger*. New York: Basic Books.

LERMAN, H. (1974) What Happens in Feminist Therapy? In *Feminist Therapy: in Search of a Theory*. Symposium: American Psychological Association meeting, New Orleans.

LIBEN, F. (1969) Minority Group Clinic Patients Pregnant out of Wedlock. *American Journal of Public Health* 59:1868–81.

LIFSHITZ, M. (1974) Quality Professionals: does training make a difference? A personal construct theory study of the issue. *British Journal of Social and Clinical Psychology* 13:183–9.

—— (1976) Girls' Identity Formation as Related to Perceptual Development of Family Structure. *Journal of Marriage and the Family* (in press).

LITMAN, G. (1975) A Microcosm of Female Stereotypes: women and alcohol. Abstract from the British Psychological Society Conference, Nottingham.

LIVINGSTONE, E. (1953) Attitudes of Women Operatives to Promotion. *Occupational Psychology*, October.

LOOFT, W. (1971) Sex Differences in the Expression of Vocational Aspirations by Elementary School Children. *Developmental Psychology* 5:366.

LOPATA, H. (1971) *Occupation Housewife*. New York: Oxford University Press.

—— (1973) Self-Identity in Marriage and Widowhood. *Sociological Quarterly* 14:407–18.

LYNN, D. (1959) A Note on Sex Differences in the Development of Masculine and Feminine Identification. *Psychological Review* 66:126–35.

MACCOBY, E. and JACKLIN, C. (1975) *The Psychology of Sex Differences*. London: Oxford University Press.

MACINTYRE, S. (1973) Classification of Social Factors by Clinicians. Unpublished manuscript.

—— (1976) Who Wants Babies? The Social Construction of Instincts. In D. Barker and S. Allen (eds.), *Sexual Divisions and Society: Process and Change*. London: Tavistock Publications.

MALMQUIST, A. and KAJ, L. (1971) Motherhood and Childlessness in Monogygous Twins. *British Journal of Psychiatry* 118:22–8.

MAON, M. (1974) Socialization of Sex-Roles in Elementary

Schools in Israel. Unpublished MA thesis, Hebrew University.

MARCHAK, M. P. (1973) The Canadian Labour Force: Jobs for Women. In M. Stephenson (ed.), *Women in Canada.* Toronto: New Press.

MASTERS, W. and JOHNSON, V. (1966) *Human Sexual Response.* Boston: Little, Brown.

MCCLELLAND, D. and WATT, N. (1968) Sex-Role Alienation in Schizophrenia. *Journal of Abnormal Psychology* 73:226–39.

MCDONALD, R. (1968) Effects of Sex, Race and Class on Self, Ideal-Self and Parental Ratings in Southern Adolescents. *Perceptual and Motor Skills* 27:15–25.

MCKEE, J. and SHERRIFFS, A. (1957) The Differential Evaluation of Males and Females. *Journal of Personality* 25:356–71.

MELTZER, H. (1943) Sex Differences in Children's Attitudes to Parents. *Journal of Genetic Psychology* 62:311–26.

MERTON, R. (1968) *Social Theory and Social Structure.* New York: Free Press.

MILLER, N. (1963) One Year After Commencement. Report No. 92. National Opinion Research Centre. Cited in Safilios-Rothschild (ed.) (1972) *Towards the Sociology of Women.* Lexington College, Massachusetts: Xerox College Publishing.

MISCHEL, H. (1974) Sex Bias in the Evaluation of Professional Achievements. *Journal of Educational Psychology* 66:157–66.

MISCHEL, W. (1970) Sex-Typing and Socialization. In *Carmichael's Manual of Child Psychology.* New York: Wiley.

MONAHAN, L., KUHN, D., and SHAVER, P. (1974) Intrapsychic Versus Cultural Explanations of the 'Fear of Success' Motive. *Journal of Personality and Social Psychology* 29:60–4.

MOORE, T. and CLAUTOUR, S. (in press) Attitudes to Life in Children and Young Adolescents. *Scandinavian Journal of Psychology.*

MUNCY, R. (1974) *Sex and Marriage in Utopian Communities.* Baltimore: Penguin Books.

MYRDAL, J. (1965) Li-Kuei-Ying, Woman Pioneer, Aged 32. In *Report from a Chinese Village.* London: Heinemann Ltd.

NASH, R. (1973) *Classrooms Observed.* London: Routledge & Kegan Paul.

NATIONAL INSTITUTE OF MENTAL HEALTH (1966) *Ad Hoc Committee on Epidemiology* October 4–5. Unpublished.

NISKANEN, P., TAMMINEN, T., and ACHTE, K. (1974) Duration of Stay in a Psychiatric Hospital during a Period of 130 Years. *Psychiatria Fennica* 4:77–81.

NORDLAND, E. (1973) *Ungdoms Holdninger i det Teknologiske Samfunn.* Oslo: Aschehoug.

NOTT, P., FRANKLIN, M., ARMITAGE, C., and GELDER, M. (1976) Hormonal Changes and Mood in the Puerperium. *British Journal of Psychiatry* 128:379–83.

NOVAK, E., JONES, G., and JONES, H. (1970) *Novak's Textbook of Gynaecology.* Baltimore: Williams & Wilkins.

NOWACKI, C. and POE, C. (1973) The Concept of Mental Health as Related to Sex of Person Perceived. *Journal of Consulting and Clinical Psychology* 40:160.

NYE, F. (1974a) Husband–Wife Relationships. In L. Hoffman and F. Nye (eds.), *Working Mothers.* San Francisco: Jossey–Bass.

—— (1974b) Effects on Mother. In L. Hoffman and F. Nye (eds.), *Working Mothers.* San Francisco: Jossey–Bass.

—— (1974c) The Sociocultural Context. In L. Hoffman and F. Nye (eds.), *Working Mothers.* San Francisco: Jossey–Bass.

NYE, F. and HOFFMAN, L. (1963a) The Sociocultural Setting. In F. Nye and L. Hoffman (eds.), *The Employed Mother in America.* Chicago: Rand McNally.

—— —— (eds.) (1963b) *The Employed Mother in America.* Chicago: Rand McNally.

OAKLEY, A. (1974a) *The Sociology of Housework.* London: Martin Robertson.

—— (1974b) *Housewife.* London: Penguin Books.

ÖDEGÄRD, O. (1963) Mental Disease in Norwegians with a High-School Background. *Acta Psychiatrica Scandinavica* 39:31–40.

O'LEARY, V. (1974) Some Attitudinal Barriers for Occupational Aspirations in Women. *Psychological Bulletin* 81:809–26.

OLSEN, D. (1969) The Measurement of Family Power by Self-Report and Behavioural Methods. *Journal of Marriage and the Family* 31:549.

PARNES, H., SHEA, J., SPITZ, R., ZELLER, F., and Associates (1970) *Dual Careers: A Longitudinal Study of Labor Market Experience of Women: Vol. 1 Manpower Research,* Monograph 24. Washington D.C.: Government Printing Office.

PATRICK, T. (1972) *Motivational and Familial Determinants of Professional Career Choice in Women*. Ph.d. dissertation, Teachers College, Columbia University, New York.

PAVENSTADT, E. (1965) Communication Conference on Mental Health in Pregnancy. National Institute of Mental Health, Bethesda, Maryland.

PERKINS, H. (1958) Factors Influencing Change in Children's Self-Concepts. *Child Development* 29 : 221–30.

PETERSON, E. (1958) The Impact of Maternal Employment on the Mother–Daughter Relationship and on the Daughter's Role-Orientation. Unpublished Ph.d. dissertation, University of Michigan.

PHETERSON, G., KIESLER, S., and GOLDBERG, P. (1971) Evaluation of the Performance of Women as a Function of their Sex, Achievement and Personal History. *Journal of Personality and Social Psychology* 19 : 114–18.

PHILLIPS, D. and SEGAL, B. (1969) Sexual Status and Psychiatric Symptoms. *American Sociological Review* 34 : 58–72.

PINES, D. (1972) Pregnancy and Motherhood : interaction between fantasy and reality. *British Journal of Medical Psychology* 45 : 333–48.

PIOTROWSKI, J. (1962) Attitudes towards Work by Women. *International Social Science Journal* 14 : 80–91.

PITT, B. (1968) 'Atypical' Depression Following Childbirth. *British Journal of Psychiatry* 114 : 1325–35.

PLANK, E. and PLANK, R. (1954) Emotional Components in Arithmetic Learning as Seen Through Autobiographies. In R. Eissler *et al.* (eds.), *The Psychoanalytic Study of the Child*. Vol. 9. New York : International Universities Press.

POLOMA, M. (1972) Role Conflict and the Married Professional Woman. In Safilios-Rothschild (ed.), *Towards a Sociology of Women*. Lexington, Massachusetts : Xerox College Publishing.

PUGH, T., JERATH, B., SCHMIDT, W., and REED, R. (1963) Rates of Mental Disease Related to Childbearing. *New England Journal of Medicine* 266 : 1224–8.

RAINWATER, L. (1968) Some Aspects of Lower Class Sexual Behaviour. *Aspects of Human Sexuality* 2 : 15–25.

RAINWATER, L., COLEMAN, R., and HANDEL, G. (1959) *Work-*

ingman's Wife: Her Personality, World and Life Style. New York: Oceana.

RAPPOPORT, A., PAYNE, D., and STEINMANN, A. (1970) Perceptual Differences between Married and Single College Women for the Concepts of Self, Ideal Woman and Man's Ideal Woman. *Journal of Marriage and the Family* 32:441–2.

RHEINGOLD, J. (1964) *The Fear of Being a Woman.* New York: Grune & Stratton.

RICHARDSON, M. (1975) Self-Concepts and Role Concepts in the Career Orientation of College Women. *Journal of Counseling of Psychology* 22:122–6.

RICHARDSON, S., GOODMAN, N., HASTORF, A., and DORNBUSCH, S. (1961) Cultural Uniformity in Reaction to Physical Disabilities. *American Sociological Review* 26:241–7.

ROBIN, A. (1962) Psychological Changes of Normal Parturition. *Psychiatric Quarterly* 36:129–50.

ROLLINS, B. and CANNON, K. (1974) Marital Satisfaction over the Family Life Cycle: a re-evaluation. *Journal of Marriage and the Family* 36:271–82.

ROLLINS, B. and FELDMAN, H. (1970) Marital Satisfaction over the Family Life Cycle. *Journal of Marriage and the Family* 32:20–8.

ROMMETVEIT, (1954) *Social Norms and Roles,* Oslo. Cited in H. Holter (1970) *Sex Roles and Social Structure.* Oslo: Universitetsforlaget.

ROSALDO, M. and LAMPHERE, L. (eds.) (1974) *Woman, Culture and Society.* Stanford, California: Stanford University Press.

ROSE, A. (1951) The Adequacy of Women's Expectations for Adult Roles. *Social Forces* 30:69–70.

ROSENFELD, C. and PERRELLA, V. (1965) Study in Mobility. *Monthly Labor Review* 88:1077–82.

ROSENGREN, W. (1961) Some Social Psychological Aspects of Delivery Room Difficulties. *Journal of Nervous and Mental Diseases* 132:515–21.

ROSENKRANTZ, P., VOGEL, S., BEE, H., BROVERMAN, I., and BROVERMAN, D. (1968) Sex-Roles Stereotypes and Self-Concepts in College Students. *Journal of Consulting and Clinical Psychology* 32:287–95.

ROSS, O. and KREITMAN, N. (1975) A Further Investigation of

222

Differences in the Suicide Rates of England and Wales and of Scotland. *British Journal of Psychiatry* 127:575–82.

ROSSER, C. and HARRIS, C. (1965) *The Family and Social Change*. London: Routledge & Kegan Paul.

ROSSI, A. (1965a) Who Wants Women Scientists? In *Women and the Scientific Professions*. Massachusetts Institute of Technology Symposium.

—— (1965b) Barriers to the Career Choice of Engineering, Medicine or Science among American Women. In J. Mattfield and C. Van Aken (eds.), *Women and the Scientific Professions*. Cambridge, Massachusetts: Massachusetts Institute of Technology Press.

—— (1972) The Roots of Ambivalence in American Women. In A. Rossi and J. Bardwick (eds.), *Readings in the Psychology of Women*. New York: Harper & Row.

ROWBOTHAM, S. (1972) *Women, Resistance and Revolution*. London: Penguin Press.

RUBIN, R. (1967) Attainment of the Maternal Role. *Nursing Research* 16:237–45.

RYDER, R. (1973) Longitudinal Data Relating Marriage Satisfaction and Having a Child. *Journal of Marriage and the Family* 35:604–6.

SALMON, P. (1970) A Psychology of Personal Growth. In D. Bannister (ed.), *Perspectives in Personal Construct Theory*. London: Academic Press.

SANDSBERG, S. (1976) Comments on Middle-aged Women's Attitudes to Themselves. Unpublished Manuscript.

SANGER, S. and ALKER, H. (1972) Dimensions of Internal–External Locus of Control and the Women's Liberation Movement. *Journal of Social Issues* 28:115–29.

SCHLESINGER, B. (1972) Family Life in the Kibbutz of Israel: Utopia gained or paradise lost? In H. Dreitzel (ed.), *Family, Marriage and the Struggle of the Sexes*. London: Collier-Macmillan.

SCHONBAR, R. (1972) Group Co-therapists and Sex-Role Identification. *American Journal of Psychotherapy* 28:539–47.

SCHWARTZ, S. (1969) Discussion of Grimm's Paper. In G. Goldman and D. Milman (eds.), *Modern Woman*. Springfield, Illinois: Charles C. Thomas.

223

SCHWENN, M. (1970) Arousal of the Motive to Avoid Success. Unpublished junior honors thesis, Harvard University. Cited in Horner (1972). *Journal of Social Issues* 28:157–75.

SCOTT, C. (1968) *The World of a Gynaecologist*. London: Oliver & Boyd.

SCULLY, D. and BART, P. (1973) A Funny Thing Happened on the Way to the Orifice: women in gynaecology textbooks. In J. Huber (ed.), *Changing Women in a Changing Society*. Chicago: University of Chicago Press.

SELIGMAN, M. (1975) *Helplessness: On Depression, Development and Death*. New York: W. H. Freeman & Co.

SHAW, M. and MCCUEN, J. (1960) The Onset of Academic Underachievement in Bright Children. *Journal of Educational Psychology* 51:103–8.

SHERMAN, J. (1971) *On the Psychology of Women: A Survey of Empirical Studies*. Springfield, Illinois: Charles C. Thomas.

SILVERMAN, C. (1968) *The Epidemiology of Depression*. Baltimore: The Johns Hopkins Press.

SIMPSON, R. and SIMPSON, I. (1963) Occupational Choice among Career-oriented College Women. *Marriage and Family Living* 23:377–83.

SINGER, J. (1966) *Daydreaming: An Introduction to the Experimental Study of Inner Experience*. New York: Random House.

SINGER, J. and ANTROBUS, J. (1972) Patterns of Daydreaming in American Subcultural Groups. In P. Sheehan (ed.), *The Function and Nature of Imagery*. New York: Academic Press.

SMART, M. and SMART, R. (1970) Self-Esteem and Social Personal Orientation of Indian 12 and 18-Year-Olds. *Psychological Reports* 27:107–15.

SOBOL, M. (1963) Commitment to Work. In F. Nye and L. Hoffman (eds.), *The Employed Mother in America*. Chicago: Rand McNally.

SPANIER, G., LEWIS., R., and COLE, C. (1975) Marital Adjustment over the Family Life Cycle: the issue of curvilinearity. *Journal of Marriage and the Family* 37:263–75.

SPENCE, J., HELMREICH, R., and STAPP, J. (1975) Ratings of Self and Peers on Sex-Role Attributes and their Relation to Self-Esteem and Conceptions of Masculinity and Femininity.

224

Journal of Personality and Social Psychology 32:29–39.

SPERLINGER, D. (1971) A Repertory Grid and Questionnaire Study of Individuals Receiving Treatment for Depression from General Practitioners. Unpublished Ph.d. thesis, University of Birmingham.

STEIN, A. and BAILEY, M. (1973) The Socialization of Achievement Orientation in Females. *Psychological Bulletin* 80:345–66.

STEIN, R. (1967–8) Social Orientations to Mental Illness in Pregnancy and Childbirth. *International Journal of Social Psychiatry* 14:56–64.

STEINMAN, H. and FOX, D. (1966) Male–Female Perceptions of the Female Role in the United States. *Journal of Psychology* 64:265–76.

STEINMANN, A. (1963) A Study of the Concept of the Feminine Role in 51 Middle-Class American Families. *Genetic Psychology Monographs* 67:275–352.

STEINMANN, A., LEVI, J., and FOX, D. (1964) Self-Concept of College Women Compared with their Concept of Ideal Woman and Men's Ideal Woman. *Journal of Counseling Psychology* 11:370–4.

STENGEL, E. (1972) *Suicide and Attempted Suicide.* Harmondsworth: Penguin Books.

STEPHENSON, M. (ed.) (1973a) *Women in Canada.* Toronto: New Press.

—— (1973b) Housewives in Women's Liberation. In M. Stephenson (ed.), *Women in Canada.* Toronto: New Press.

STINNET, N., COLLINS, J., and MONTEGOMERY, J. (1970) Marital Need Satisfaction of Older Husbands and Wives. *Journal of Marriage and the Family* 32:428–34.

STRICKER, G. (1977) Implications of Research for Psychotherapeutic Treatment of Women. *American Psychologist* 32:14–22.

TANGRI, S. (1972) Determinants of Occupational Role Innovation among College Women. *Journal of Social Issues* 28:177–99.

TAVRIS, C. (1973) Who Likes Women's Liberation – and Why?: the case of the unliberated liberals. *Journal of Social Issues* 29:175–98.

THOMAS, E. and BIDDLE, B. (1966) The Nature and History of Role Theory. In B. Biddle and E. Thomas (eds.), *Role Theory: Concepts and Research*. New York: Wiley.

THOMPSON, L. (1942) Attitudes of Primiparae as Observed in a Prenatal Clinic. *Mental Hygiene* 26:243–56.

THOMPSON, S. and BENTLER, P. (1973) A Developmental Study of Gender Constancy and Parent Preference. *Archives of Sexual Behavior* 2:379–85.

TIGER, L. and SHEPHER, J. (1975) *Women in the Kibbutz*. New York: Harcourt Brace Jovanovich.

TIME (1972) March 20:89.

TOOMEY, D. (1971) Conjugal Roles and Social Networks in an Urban Working-Class Sample. *Human Relations* 24:417–32.

TOWNSEND, P. (1963) *The Family Life of Old People*. London: Penguin Books.

TRESEMER, D. (1973) Fear of Success: popular but unproven. In C. Travis (ed.), *The Female Experience*. California: Delmar.

TURNER, B. and TURNER, C. (1974) Evaluations of Women and Men among Black and White College Students. *Sociological Quarterly* 15:442–56.

VEEVERS, J. (1973) Voluntarily Childless Wives: an exploratory study. *Sociology and Social Research* 3:356–66.

VEROFF, J. and FELD, S. (1970) *Marriage and Work in America*. New York: Van Nostrand–Reinhold.

VEROFF, J., WILCOX, S., and ATKINSON, J. (1953) The Achievement Motive in High School and College Age Women. *Journal of Abnormal and Social Psychology* 48:108–19.

VOGEL, S., BROVERMAN, I., BROVERMAN, D., CLARKSON, F., and ROSENKRANTZ, P. (1970) Maternal Employment and Perception of Sex-Roles among College Students. *Developmental Psychology* 3:384–91.

WARHEIT, G., HOLZER, C., and SCHWAB, J. (1973) An Analysis of Social Class and Racial Differences in Depressive Symptomatology: a community study. *Journal of Health and Social Behavior* 14:291–9.

WASSERMAN, E. (1973) Changing Aspirations of College Women. *Journal of American College Health Association* 21:333–5.

WEBSTER, M., Jr. and SOBIESZEK, B. (1974) *Sources of Self-Evaluation: A Formal Theory of Significant Others and Social Influence.* New York: Wiley.

WEISS, P. (1961) Some Aspects of Feminity. Unpublished Ph.d. dissertation, University of Colorado.

WEISS, R. and SAMELSON, N. (1958) Social Roles of American Women: their contributions to a sense of usefulness and importance. *Marriage and Family Living* 20:358-66.

WEISSMAN, M. and PAYKEL, E. (1974) *The Depressed Woman.* Chicago: University of Chicago Press.

WHITE, T. (1973) Autonomy in Work: are women any different? In M. Stephenson (ed.), *Women in Canada.* Toronto: New Press.

WHITFIELD, W. (1976) His and Her Housework. *Spare Rib* 45:6-7.

WILMOTT, P. and YOUNG, M. (1967) *Family and Class in a London Suburb.* London: Nel Mentor.

WILSNACK, S. (1973) Sex Role Identity in Female Alcoholism. *Journal of Abnormal Psychology* 82:253-61.

WOLF, T. (1973) Effects of Live Modeled Sex-Inappropriate Play Behaviour in a Naturalistic Setting. *Developmental Psychology* 9:120-3.

WOLF, T. (1974) Response Consequences to Televised Modeled Sex-Inappropriate Play Behaviour. *Developmental Psychology*.

WYER, R. and WEATHERLEY, D. (1965) Social Role Aggression and Academic Success. *Journal of Personality and Social Psychology* 1:645-9.

WYLIE, R. (1975) *The Self Concept.* Lincoln: University of Nebraska Press.

YEARBOOK OF NEUROLOGY, PSYCHIATRY AND NEUROSURGERY (1964-5) R. P. Mackay *et al.* (eds.). Chichester: Wiley and Sons.

ZAJICEK, E. (1976) Development of Women Having their First Child. Proceedings of annual conference of British Psychological Society, York.

ZAZZO, R. (1956) Le Bestiaire. *Enfance* 1:65-84.

ZEMLICK, M. and WATSON, R. (1953) Maternal Attitudes of Acceptance and Rejection during and after Pregnancy. *American Journal of Orthopsychiatry* 23:570-84.

ZERETSKY, E. (1976) *Capitalism, the Family and Personal Life.* London: Pluto Press.

ZISSIS, C. (1962) The Relationship of Selected Variables to Career–Marriage Plans of University Freshman Women. Ph.d. thesis, University of Michigan.

ZIV, A., SIPSTEIN, D., and LITAN, M. (1973) Sex Differences in Sex-Role Stereotypes among Israeli Adolescents. *Hachinuch* (Hebrew) 45:65–9.

Name Index

229

231

Subject Index

234

236